'Lisa and Alan's masterplan of solid marketing strategies is what all businesses need at this time. Don't go into the future without it.'

Ali Brown, *Founder and CEO of The Trust: the new,*
premier global network for women entrepreneurs
generating 7- and 8-figure revenues.

'This intriguing book turns conventional wisdom upside down, stressing the need to create disruption and exploit volatility in providing value to customers and clients globally.'

Jonah Berger, *Marketing Professor, Wharton School*
at the University of Pennsylvania and author of
Invisible Influence, Contagion, *and* The Catalyst

'I tried to skim the intro but ended up devouring the entire book! Just when I thought I've seen it all they show me new ways of thinking and reminding me of all their great historical skills. The case studies alone are priceless.'

Noah Kagan, *CEO of AppSumo.com*

ALAN WEISS AND LISA LARTER

MASTERFUL MARKETING

How to dominate your market with a value-based approach

BLOOMSBURY BUSINESS
LONDON · OXFORD · NEW YORK · NEW DELHI · SYDNEY

BLOOMSBURY BUSINESS
Bloomsbury Publishing Plc
50 Bedford Square, London, WC1B 3DP, UK
29 Earlsfort Terrace, Dublin 2, Ireland

BLOOMSBURY, BLOOMSBURY BUSINESS and the Diana logo are trademarks
of Bloomsbury Publishing Plc

First published in Great Britain 2022

A catalogue record for this book is available from the British Library

Library of Congress Cataloging-in-Publication data has been applied for

ISBN: 978-1-4729-9468-4; eBook: 978-1-4729-9467-7

2 4 6 8 10 9 7 5 3 1

Typeset by Deanta Global Publishing Services, Chennai, India
Printed and bound in Great Britain by CPI Group (UK) Ltd, Croydon CR0 4YY

To find out more about our authors and books visit www.bloomsbury.com
and sign up for our newsletters

OTHER WORKS BY ALAN WEISS

Organizational Consulting
Our Emperors Have No Clothes
Process Consulting
The Consulting Bible (also in Portuguese)
The DNA of Leadership (with Myron Beard)
The Global Consultant
The Great Big Book of Process Visuals
The Innovation Formula (with Mike Robert) (also in German, Italian)
The Language of Success (with Kim Wilkerson)
The Modern Trusted Advisor (with Nancy MacKay)
The Resilience Advantage (with Richard Citrin)
The Son of the Great Big Book of Process Visuals
The Talent Advantage (with Nancy MacKay)
The Ultimate Consultant
The Unofficial Guide to Power Management
The Power of Strategic Commitment (with Josh Leibner and Gershon Mader)
Threescore and More
Thrive!
Value Based Fees
Who's Got Your Back?
Your Legacy is Now

Podcast Series: Alan Weiss's The Uncomfortable Truth®
Video Series: Alan Weiss's The Writing on the Wall®

Newsletters: Balancing Act: The 1% Solution®
Million Dollar Consulting® Mindset
Alan Weiss's Monday Morning Memo®

Blog: Contrarian Consulting

CONTENTS

INTRODUCTION

'Masterful' means 'powerful and able to attract others'. And 'marketing' is an activity intended to help sell products and services.

Any questions?

Well, you should have some and our intention is to answer them within the following pages.

We've all been exposed to brilliant marketing:

- The giant hammer smashing the screen with 'Big Brother' on it, signalling Apple taking on IBM in their Super Bowl commercial from 1984;
- The 'rinse and repeat' direction on shampoo bottles which doubled use of the product without a penny of marketing investment (despite the fact that no one needs to shampoo twice);
- The advice that certain cigarettes are better for you than others – even for pregnant women – decades ago, as attested by 'doctors';
- The modern role of 'influencers' on social media;

- The power of sayings and memes: 'Don't leave home without it.'

But marketing doesn't need to be as grand and global as these examples. Effective marketing for your firm, no matter what its size, is incremental and daily. How you attract people (we call them 'browsers'), how you convert them to customers, how you capitalize on that conversion with expanded business and referral business is what strong, growing businesses do daily.

Our focus is on *value* and creating need, not merely responding to 'wants'. That's the difference between being seen as a unique source judged for return on investment (ROI) and not solely a commodity being judged on price. We'll also demonstrate that not every customer is a good customer, not every lead is a worthwhile lead, and how to tell the difference.

In a global, electronic, volatile age you may be prone to think that you have to shout louder, appear all over and generally be calling attention to yourself. But that's to be a part of the herd that is doing that every day, rumbling across the plains, raising a cloud of dust. We want to help you stand out in a crowd by leaving the crowd. We want you to be easily found by your ideal buyers and to impress them with the value of a relationship immediately, whether in person or remotely. How can we do that? Well, we've both done it with our global client base and we've helped others to do it with our coaching and support daily. We're happy to share all of that in this book to accelerate your growth through truly Masterful Marketing.

Join us on this journey of helping others.

Alan Weiss, East Greenwich, RI
Lisa Larter, Calgary, Canada
September 2022

THE GENESIS OF VALUE

THE DIFFERENCE BETWEEN 'WANTS' AND 'NEEDS'

One fine day, about 35 years ago, I made the last 'cold call' purchase in my memory. A woman I didn't know called me and this was the ensuing conversation:

Woman: Is this Alan Weiss?

Me: Yes. (Could have been my doctor or the bank.)

Woman: Do you drive a Mercedes 450 SLC?

Me: Yes. (I figured it was a recall or warranty issue.)

Woman: How would you like to own one of the first car phones in New England?

Me: (After a three-second pause) How fast can you get here?

We want you to understand three basic concepts right off the bat:

1 We know what we want, but not always what we need.

2 Logic makes us think but emotion makes us act.

3 A luxury is only a luxury until used once, after which it's a necessity.

Not long after the installation I was talking to London while driving with my wife. This was via a hard-wired regular handset with a holder on the dashboard. After the call, I said, 'Pretty poor reception.' She said, 'Alan, you're talking to London from your car, shut up!'

Even people who are clearly in touch with their 'wants' are not always willing to do what's needed to achieve the want. You may want a new car, but you need to save the money to finance it. You may want to be the market leader, but you're unwilling to take even prudent risks to stand out in a crowd.

People talk about wanting fame, business growth, a stronger brand and so on, but often they don't invest what's needed: time, money, hard work, finding the right advice and so forth.

In Figure 1.1 you can see what we call 'the value distance'. The greater the need you can create, as distanced from mere 'wants', the more valuable your products and service. If that distance is a few inches, who cares? If you simply cater to the want, you're a commodity and price sensitive but if you show the greater need that can be met, you're invaluable.

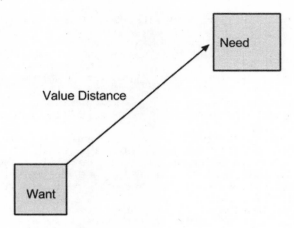

FIGURE I.I The Value Distance

MASTERFUL INSIGHTS

Marketing is the creation of need into which you can position your products and service as the best alternatives.

The genesis of value is about demonstrating to buyers that they need more than they think they do and/or that they haven't even considered larger issues.

CASE STUDY

The Vice President of Operations asked that we conduct a leadership retreat over three days for his top team of ten people. Instead of simply citing a $20,000 fee, we asked *why* he wanted it.

He told us that his team was not making decisions consistent with the firm's strategy, or their annual business plan, and weren't sufficiently sharing information with each other. We asked if he felt that way about all ten.

'Well, no,' he admitted, 'only about half of them, but I thought this would make for a good team-building exercise.'

'Have you considered that these ten have very different tenures here and that they might not be equally conversant in the company strategy and/or that they feel it might conflict with your business plan?' we asked.

He admitted that was possible. We began by coaching each of the ten individually and then conducting a strategy session with the vice president and his team over the course of a single day. We also provided a 60-day follow-up as advisors.

That fee was $140,000 and the client was delighted.

We all need to get in the habit of habitually creating value for others. To do this well and consistently, remember that decisions come in 'chains' and we seldom enter at the top or the bottom. For example, our decision to buy a new car implies that we've already decided on new (not used), a car (not a truck or bike), one (not several) and to buy (not lease, rent or steal). Those are a lot of decisions already and following decisions would involve models, colours and so forth.

When you ask *why*, you go up the chain to broader and more valuable needs. When you ask *how*, you go down the chain to implementation and less value. In marketing and promotion, *always go up, not down*! This is why there is strategic and tactical advertising. Strategic promotion accentuates the need and the *what*: Buy a Ford F150 pickup because it can take care of all your needs, on road or off. Wear a Brioni suit because you'll be seen as successful and having good taste. Tactical promotion highlights the fact that the local Ford dealership has a special sale this weekend or that Saks has the latest Brioni styles for spring.

People will often use the words 'want' and 'need' interchangeably, but they mean quite different things in marketing. When someone has a 'calling' (a nurse, fire-fighter, clergy, architect and so forth) they not only want to protect others or build houses or help the sick, but they really *need* to do so to fulfil themselves. When someone says, 'I want to get out of this business', they don't mean they really need to do so but that it would be a desire, were they able to do so. Let's now examine how emotion really generates action and why people change in accordance with their own best interests.

THE PERSONAL ROI EQUATION

The usual definition of branding is that it is the uniform representation of value but we prefer a more pragmatic explanation: It's how people think of you when you're not around. Corporate CEOs do not have to be looking at McKinsey & Company to know they exist and can provide expert strategy help. Most people don't have to look at an Armani ad to know this high-end label represents elegant, tasteful clothing. If logic makes us think and emotions urge us to action, ideally, a brand should strike at emotions. In other words: What's in it for me?

People can't choose you if they don't know you exist, or if told of you they've never heard of you, or if when you're explained to them you don't impress. Potential buyers have to *trust* you. That need creation which we established was the basis of marketing implies consistent and impressive value. This is the antithesis of price-sensitive commodities, where one product or service is undifferentiated from the next and the only salient factor in decision making is price.

The more value you bring – the personal ROI equation for the buyer – means that the more value you deliver, the more you're recommended, the more value you can deliver to new people and the more they recommend you. I call this 'the chain reaction of attraction'®. It means that you can grow exponentially (ten people each mentioning you to ten people) rather than merely arithmetically (one person mentioning you to one other person).

Consider this sequence: browse, consider, buy, build. Your prospective buyers will want to become acquainted with your value. In professional services, for example, this can't be a 'test drive' as in an auto dealer. Prospects need to read or listen to or experience your approaches for free. Think of eBooks, or podcasts, or blog posts, or newsletters and so forth.

MASTERFUL INSIGHTS

Every sale is actually and potentially three sales: the immediate payment, referral business and expansion business. Most people leave one or two of the three on the table.

Traditional ROI is about WIIFM (what's in it for me?). But today, it's joined by SWIIFT (see what's in it for them). People change (in other words, going from 'no' to 'yes') if it's in their best interests. A great many people come to me wanting a favour, telling me how important it is to them, but failing to even try to show me what's in it for me. While I don't always demand reciprocity, it does make the decision easier and quicker, however!

CASE STUDY

I was coaching a woman who was overwhelmed. Her time was booked every day with no room to market or explore or create, let alone relax. I found out why very quickly. The basic question she asked herself whenever she was approached was, 'Can I help this person?' If the answer was 'yes', she helped them regardless of their ability to pay or the amount of the fee.

I told her I asked myself a different question. I asked, 'What's in it for me?' If that was appealing — and it didn't have to be monetary, although that always helps — then it was an easy decision but also an ironclad way to control my own time.

THE STRANGER ZONE

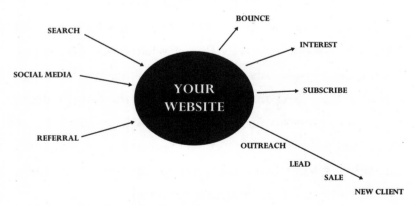

FIGURE 1.2 The Stranger Zone

Although websites aren't usually sales tools or closers (in the corporate world; they can be in retail), they are important in the 'browsing to buying' continuum. This real estate has to display tremendous credibility and provide free value if browsers are to become buyers.

Here's an example of this 'stranger zone' and subsequent conversion in practice.

CASE STUDY

A client of ours invested in aligning his website brand with his actual skills and abilities and started to create regular content to add value for others. Within four months of his new brand and website release, he received several new enquiries about his services, which resulted in five new buyers.

The average buyer who works with him invests $10,000 a month for a three-year period. The total lifetime value of these enquiries that turned into buyers is approximately $1.6 million in revenue. Our client said since he improved his brand and focused on delivering regular valuable content, he has been able to attract more enquiries from the right type of client, the conversations are much easier and the speed at which they say 'yes' is significantly faster.

Behind every corporate objective is a personal objective (what's in it for them). If a prospect says she needs to have better, more co-operative teamwork, it's as if she's weary of wasting her time playing referee among teams acting like warring parties. Hunt out – or create if you must – those kinds of individual benefits which will accelerate the browsing to the buying.

We call the website the 'stranger zone' because it should be welcoming those people who don't know you well or at all, but where they can participate in the value you've created for free.

They should be thinking, 'What would I be getting if I actually hired this person?'

THE PRESSURES AFFECTING VALUE
Value is key, right from the outset, but it's difficult to 'hear' it amid all the current noise, which is probably worse than ever before.

The internet cliché that no one knows you're a dog on the internet is actually profound. One of the problems is that everyone's opinion becomes for them (and others) a 'fact'. There are people promoting their marketing expertise on social media platforms who have never marketed anything themselves successfully – except their purported marketing 'expertise'. The question becomes: Do you want the ski instructor who sits in the lodge drinking brandy while telling you what to do when you go up the lift in the morning by yourself, or the one who goes up with you and skis 10 yards in front of you, demonstrating what to do?

MASTERFUL INSIGHTS

Never accept coaching or any kind of advice from anyone who hasn't done what you seek to do.

Moreover, social media presents huge waves of confirmation bias opportunity, where you can listen only to those who agree with you, no matter how wrong they may be, and ignore all those who disagree with you, no matter how right they may be. (This is also the basis of 'conspiracy theories', where people support each other in the absence of all evidence or even in the face of great evidence to the contrary.)

One downside is that people feel they have nothing to add to the loud conversations and withhold their value or think poorly of it. The issue here is about not caring what people may think.

As you can see in Figure 1.3, we need respect more than 'affection' or affiliation. Don't seek love from your clients, seek it from your family. Or get a dog (I have two dogs). As a marketer, you want to be seen as a trusted advisor, who is respected and liked. If you're merely liked but not

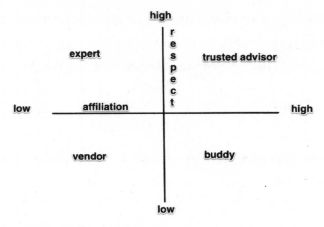

FIGURE 1.3 Respect and Affiliation

respected, you're a 'buddy', and if you're respected but not liked, you're an arm's-length expert (think of an expert witness at a trial). If you're neither, you're simply a vendor and no value attaches to that status because you're merely a commodity and price sensitive.

So leave your vanity and need for affection at home. Don't be one of those speakers who looks for all '1 os' on the evaluation sheets, or doesn't believe in success unless there's a standing ovation. Focus on the client, not you. *How is the client better off after you walk away? What's in their best interests?*

Even the technology platforms that do prove the opportunity for real value are changing at a lightning pace (as you would expect). Thus, we have to deliver our value diversely: in text, video, audio, virtually, in newsletters, on blogs, in webinars, at live events and so forth. The value you portray in the 'browse to close' sequence must be commensurate with the fees you wish to charge.

You have to invest in your projected value. Never be afraid to give it away out of fear that the recipients will no longer need you. I've published over 60 books yet people come to me for expensive experiences, coaching and training.

No one ever learned to ride a bike by reading a book.

CASE STUDY

Louis Vuitton is a great example of a luxury brand that demonstrates value. They operate beautiful retail stores, regularly offer browsers water or a glass of champagne while they shop, they have exceptional white-glove service and when you buy, the quality of the packaging is outstanding. LV sells a high-priced product and they support the entire buyer's journey and experience in a way that is aligned with the price point they are selling: you do not expect to use self-checkout and pay five cents for a bag as you do when you shop at Walmart.

YOU GET WHAT YOU PAY FOR

Why do people pay for a Bentley when almost any car can provide transportation? Why wear a Breitling watch when any timepiece (or just your smartphone) can tell the time? (My kids would say why wear a watch at all? I tell them it's an accessory, jewellery, and I'm not gaining any points by wearing my iPhone on my wrist.)

We've established that it's emotion that drives action. In fact, emotion drives *urgency*. The more 'urgent' we feel something is, the faster we want to act. It's not difficult to consider that 'urgent' can be obvious to all: the need for an operation, or to attend a family event, or to make the final flight home. But 'urgent' can also mean that the individual simply wants immediate gratification and prefers not to wait. Thus, it can be 'urgent' to start a new business initiative, buy a new outfit, play golf on a new course.

CASE STUDY

Recently, I needed a type of wrench that wasn't in my toolkit to assemble a new product. I visited the hardware store and found three identical-looking wrenches at different price points. While they all looked the same, I purchased the most expensive. I figured it was probably made of better material, which justified the higher price.

Many businesses, in tough times, employ a counter-intuitive strategy. They *raise* their prices. Consumers feel there's a higher value inherent in the higher price and clear the shelves of the more expensive item while not touching the lower-priced, 'mediocre' item.

This is a very real phenomenon and it looks like this:

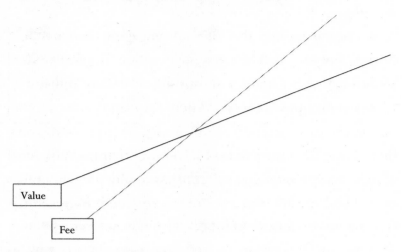

FIGURE 1.4 Value Follows Fee

As you can see, fee traditionally follows perceived value but the lines will eventually cross. They cross where there is a strong brand, creating strong emotions and urgency. Thus, people want the Brioni suit, the Breitling watch, the Bentley car. And they want it now. This means that Masterful Marketing is about creating irresistible experiences, feelings, beliefs and brand identity. When my kids were old enough to have a car, my son told his sister, 'Don't worry, Dad would never buy us an embarrassing old car because in the remote event his car is being serviced, Mom's car is with her somewhere and the SUV is out of gas, he won't want to be seen driving our car unless it's decent.'

He was right.

> ## MASTERFUL INSIGHTS
>
> Marketing is the dynamic of engaging customers in something that creates an emotional appeal and comfort, and that they want now, not later, and that they want other people to know they have.

Executives don't just call for McKinsey & Company because of their track record and size, they know they can brag that they called in the 'best'. It doesn't matter if McKinsey is too expensive, takes too long, and sends in junior people, because they are proud of engaging them. This is why so many restaurants with huge names and inferior food don't just survive, they thrive. Or as Yankees legend Yogi Berra said, 'Nobody goes there anymore, it's too crowded.' People believe they get what they pay for. They want to be seen and heard by others as being 'hip' and learned and 'in'.

Let's turn to some popular beliefs about what that means and how best to get there or not get there at all.

2

INTERNET MARKETING FUNNELS
ARE NOT THE ANSWER

THERE IS NOTHING PASSIVE ABOUT PASSIVE INCOME
We all turn to the internet today as the easiest way to market.
The problem is that the easiest way to fly would be to jump
off a roof and flap our arms. Some people have actually tried
it. It's not the fall that kills you, it's the sudden stop.

The Ponzi scheme was the work of one Charles Ponzi
who, in the 1920s, promised a 50 per cent return within
45 days or a 100 per cent return in 90 days, through the
purchase of discounted postal reply coupons from other
countries. (I'm not making this up.) He used new money to
pay back prior investors and got away with it for a year until
it collapsed. The cost to investors in money lost was $250
million in today's equivalent. He ended his life in poverty
and illness and died in a charity hospital in Brazil in 1949.

Of course, we never learn our lessons and Bernie Madoff
carried off the exact same scam until 2008, about 90 years
later. The cost to investors, before efforts at compensation
in today's dollars: $19 billion.

You'll find equivalent scams on social media platforms. Pyramid schemes today (also known as multi-level marketing, network marketing and so forth) work on the same principle, except the putative product is detergent or phone cards. But after the originators begin the solicitation for 'distributorships' and the first or second level of 'investors' make their money, subsequent investors will lose theirs because there simply are not enough (gullible) people to continue to fund the scheme. By the time it collapses, the originators are long gone and setting up a new pyramid — perhaps selling discounted postal reply coupons!

If you want to build a long-term, sustainable brand of quality which attracts 'evergreen' clients, there is no substitute for quality and honesty. You need best practices, not shortcuts. (In track and field, you could take a shortcut and run across the middle of the oval instead of running around it, but you can't win that way, you'll simply be thrown out.) Best practices (running on the inside, leaning correctly, saving for a finishing 'kick') include:

- Proactive and frequent contact with customers;
- Visibility in the 'public square' with opinions and value;
- Distributing your intellectual property through diverse channels;
- Expanding your base nationally and globally;
- Creating a body of great work.

> ## MASTERFUL INSIGHTS
>
> A brand is how people think about you when you're not around.

If you want to get rich, do great work, don't pursue 'great' shortcuts. If you can accomplish that, referral business becomes the norm. *This is probably the weakest pursuit of most business owners and entrepreneurs we encounter — the inability to consistently request referral business.* When you have a great track record and delight clients, there are two dimensions of referrals that ensue:

1 You request referrals and are given them faithfully each time. This is the gold standard.
2 You receive unsolicited referrals from delighted clients. This is the platinum standard.

Instead of chasing business, business chases you! Your buyers become your biggest advocates and client 'evangelism' provides input to your sales pipeline. Modern marketing is all about evangelism, which means first you need grateful and appreciative clients who are all too eager to share their happiness in working with you.

The questions are always: What will improve the buyer's/client's/customer's condition? What's in the best interest of the buyer/client/customer?

Masterful Marketing is about creating constant value generation. Value becomes reciprocal. It's an appeal to people's emotions and the creation of urgency. This is a critical differentiator: Your mindset cannot be 'How can I make a quick buck and lure people into some immediate scheme?' It has to be 'How can I provide value that will create long-term relationships?' leading to:

1   Immediate business.
2   Expansion business.
3   Referral business.

I call this 'thinking of the fourth sale first', the antithesis of the 'shortcut' to quick revenue.

CASE STUDY

Many years ago, I invested $15,000 in working with one of my first coaches. This coach believed that it was easier to sell more to an existing buyer than it was to continuously find new buyers. The approach this coach recommended to me at the time was to sell a $7 eBook. The eBook was high value, and the price point was low, and this coach believed that if someone bought the eBook, it would be easy to upsell them to another offer.

I bought in and invested a ton of time and effort in the creation of this eBook and marketing funnel. Over a six-month period, I sold over 1,000 e-books and then, I came to my senses. I had invested $15,000 in this coach, even more in the set-up of this sales funnel, to generate $7,000 in sales from people who were not my ideal buyers.

I had bought into a gimmick that didn't work. As soon as I realized what I had done, I went back to my original strategy of trying to attract one new client each month who would work with me long term and completely changed the trajectory of my business. If it's too good to be true, it likely isn't true that it will work.

'Passive income' is not about finding quick ways to lure prospects into schemes that are only good for you. Help the client to 'get rich quick' based on your ethical and legal help and you'll do just fine.

INTERNET MARKETING TRENDS ARE JUST TRENDS

Internet marketing was designed to sell you concepts that rarely work and always leave you feeling as though you're not good enough. Aggressive 'insider' tips or spam tactics to build your list and try to sell your services don't work, they only serve to degrade your reputation and expertise. Cold calling doesn't work in almost all sales situations, and even when it does work, it's an exception and not a business-builder long term. When was the last time you bought from someone you don't know who unexpectedly called or wrote to you? Most buying today is done through word of mouth and peer reference and the research is consistent about this.*

'Trends' represent general directions of popular things, issues, offerings and so forth but it also means 'fashion' and trends can be deceptive and very short-lived. When you choose an attractive trend, you've chosen to follow someone else. That's why so much is derivative today. Remember the enormous bestseller, *Chicken Soup for the Soul*, which was actually not a 'book' but a compilation of 101 feel-good stories? It was a huge hit, which fostered an 'industry' of books (*Chicken Soup for the Teen Soul*), products, manuals, learning systems and so forth. The authors, whom I knew before, during and after their success, Mark Victor Hansen and Jack Canfield, are superb marketers. They created this brilliant approach but then a boatload of people tried to follow the trend. I received requests every day from people proposing to write *Turkey Broth for the Arteries* and wanting to use my stories, which I had to give up possession of to allow them to copyright them.

---

*See for example Jonah Berger's work at the Wharton School, who estimates that only 4 per cent of peer referral occurs over the internet. See his books *Contagion* (Simon & Schuster, 2013) and *Invisible Influence* (Simon & Schuster, 2016).

Thanks, but no thanks, and not one of them was successful. Derivatives seldom are. The first people to jump on someone else's trend may manage to hang on, like Lyft with Uber, but the later arrivals will bounce off and hit the pavement. UPS has emulated what FedEx created, though not as well, and DHL had to drop out of the American market altogether.

How about Periscope, the live streaming on Twitter that was supposed to be the enormously effective 'new' way to market? It came complete with random people who would drop obscene comments into your narrative! As this is written, Clubhouse is the big new trend (it won't be by the time you read this). I tried it so that I could talk intelligently about it to my clients, as a guest 'on stage' found that it was raucous, self-congratulatory, noisy and had an irrelevant audience. It was like a bad bar, where the bouncer had gone home, the door was left open, the food was awful and the liquor cheap.

MASTERFUL INSIGHTS

Don't ask whether a trend can make you money, ask if it can be seized as a benefit to your ideal buyers.

The question to ask is this: Does this trend work for me and my audience? For instance, using Zoom is a no-brainer for my audience and prospects in a world of increasing acceptance of remote value. However, the far more important question is this: What trends can I *create?*

We've begun trends such as value-based fees replacing time-based fees in consulting; internet marketing strategies rather than merely implementation; finding the ideal buyer for your value and creating marketing gravity for that person; and creating integrated promotion and bonuses for successful book launches. Think of 'fashion' and trend setting. Some people are slaves to fashion, others master fashion as appropriate for them. I saw a woman with her left leg in a cast dressed in a miniskirt and sweater, on crutches, with a four-inch heel on her right foot. That's downright dangerous, beyond being a fashion slave. I've seen men with baseball caps on backwards shielding their eyes with their hands on sunny days. That might not be dangerous, but it's certainly dumb and looks foolish.

For our clients, we want to be seen as professional, in our attire, our language and in our promotion. You may not feel it necessary to buy Manolo Blahnik or Christian Louboutin heels, but you don't want to be seen in plastic ones either. You don't need the most expensive website on the internet, but neither do you want one with typos, poor-quality photos or pages 'under construction'.

Be aware when a trend is actually more than a trend. Two decades after the launch of Facebook, some people still look at social media platforms as part of a trend! They have ignored or failed to see (perhaps because that hand is shielding their eyes from the sun) the economic, social, technical and seismic shifts that have permanently altered the landscape.

Remember, once is an accident, twice is a coincidence and three times is a pattern. People laugh at the true story of the head of the US patent office, Charles Holland Duell, who said in 1899 that the patent office would soon have to close because everything that could be invented had been invented! Yet, periodically over the past ten years,

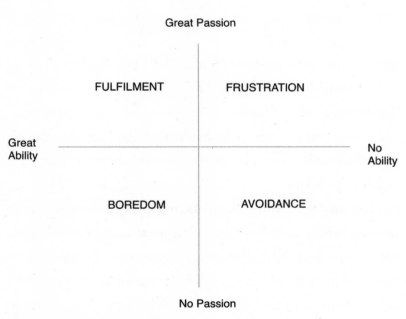

FIGURE 2.1 Passion and Ability

investment advisors who want my business have advised me to sell my holdings in Apple because it couldn't possibly maintain its growth. (I purchased Apple at $17 per share and have been through something like 20 splits since.)

With passion and ability, you can create trends and objectively assess current ones. That's a fulfilling process. If you don't have that ability then you'll be continually frustrated as you miss opportunity or jump on wagons going nowhere (per rock, anyone?). If you have the ability but not the passion to pursue or create promising trends, then you're bored and need to find other work. And if you have neither the ability nor the passion, you're avoiding accountability.

HOW TO KNOW WHICH INTERNET MARKETING CONCEPTS WORK FOR YOU

Marketing is like keeping fit: there is always the next step, you are never 'done'. Transactional and continual, it's about acquiring leads, converting prospects to clients and *sustaining* clients.

Many of the internet marketing programs were built on the premise of 'problem-solution-new problem-new solution'. Ironically, the modern internet focus on this harkens back to the 1950s when you were supposed to focus on prospects' 'pain points'. This is no longer valid, unless you believe that hamster wheels create forward progress. There is the constant 'upsell' of new problems, new solutions, not unlike modern video games (try playing Candy Crush and rising up the ratings without continually investing). This creates a 'bait and switch' wariness on the part of the potential clients and a focus on making money, not providing value. It simply doesn't work today because:

- Innovation is the market-dominating strategy, not problem solving;
- Most organizations (and individuals) have become highly adept at problem solving using modern tools and methodologies;
- 'Lean' and 'agile' practices have created the equivalent of rapid response to problem solving;
- Problem *prevention* is what saves money, time, injury and reputation.

CASE STUDY

At one point, I employed the firm of a technical guy who became enamoured with people who provided four free videos on internet marketing and then introduced a fifth 'with all the answers' for a fee, along with expensive coaching options. This became his primary goal, to create and sell these videos. It turns out, of course, that the videos merely taught others how to sell further videos. In other words, it was just a variation on the pyramid schemes.

'What value are you providing?' I asked him.

'I'm making money, that's the point,' he informed me.

I fired him and his firm. He still doesn't have that video and he's worse off than he was ten years ago.

This is a relationship business, hence the accent on referrals and peer-to-peer references. We see people all the time overly concerned about which shade of grey to use on their website (we are not making this up) or which of a dozen subtitles is best. The truth is that neither the colour nor the one line of wording will make a big difference: the brand is the issue, the visibility is the issue, the value being provided is the issue.

The point in marketing is your ability to transfer credibility and trust to others. People who already use your services may love you, but people considering you do not. You don't want to create love, you want to create respect.

Lisa Larter coined the term 'invitation marketing' years ago. She coupled her idea for an event with a great location and included photos of the venue. Within 24 hours, it was a sellout. There was no sales page or sophisticated copy, no sophisticated image or even a shopping cart for ordering. There was simply an idea and invitation for a special experience.

Invitation marketing can be likened to 'destination weddings'. Alan holds 'destination experiences' from Bora Bora to Dubrovnik, Mykonos to Melbourne. He maintains that there are three keys to attracting people:

1 Brand.
2 Perceived Value.
3 Venue.

He says you can sometimes succeed with two of the three, never with just one, and all three are the guarantee of success.

There's another key element here that you need to master as you build your marketing efforts. Alan has trademarked The Chain Reaction of Attraction®. While the internet purports to reach huge amounts of people, the key for you is to reach a significant amount of ideal buyers.

MASTERFUL INSIGHTS

'Reach' is the total number of people on your list times the quality – how many are buyers or recommenders?

When you attract people who themselves have significant communities of followers consistent with your ideal buyers you are exponentially growing your 'reach'. Large numbers of people on a list are irrelevant if they are not buyers. The internet can provide numbers but not necessarily quality.

The problem arises when you attract 'browsers' who you want to convert to buyers and the browsers are incapable of buying. The irony is that the internet seems to offer a huge return on time investment because of the vast potential numbers of followers, likes, friends and whatever, but this isn't a numbers game, it's a quality pursuit. That's why we don't advertise on motorway billboards or in the sports sections of the daily paper.

In the classic Broadway play *Avenue Q* there is a satirical song called 'The Internet Was Made for Porn'. The point is that the free speech and wide dissemination possible with the internet also makes it a key leverage point for the purveyors of porn and other distasteful material. Note that 'social media' platforms are called exactly that because they are not 'business media platforms'.

The aggressive advice you hear from internet 'experts' usually only puts money – yours – in their pockets.

WHY YOU SHOULD AVOID USING AGGRESSIVE TACTICS ONLINE

'Scrape, Spam and Sell' does not work. Scrape email addresses from folks you have subscribed to or connected to on LinkedIn and add them to your mailing list. Don't spam people via email or direct messages with your pitch and stop trying to sell a solution to a problem that hasn't been discovered through conversation. The buyer is in control of the sales process today, not you. When you resort to these types of practices, you damage your credibility and expertise, and come across as desperate for business. Even worse, when you pitch someone blindly without doing any research on them, you look like a fool. Stop selling too soon and selling the same way to everyone you can reach.

This has probably happened to you: I helped a woman with her web pages and overall promotion, then narrated her demonstration video for her. She was a terrific client and a top talent. Next thing I know, I'm informed several times daily that there is a new post on LinkedIn on a thread where I'm mentioned. It was her talking about her work, but the technical team she hired simply put #alanweiss – and two dozen other well-known people with strong followings – on her posting. This is 'tag spam'. She knew nothing about it. When I told her, she immediately agreed to take those names off, but not before she fired her technical team: brands are far too important to allow them to be tarnished with cheap tactics.

The future is about allowing the buyer to buy and evangelism. It's not about 'clicks' or 'openings' or volume of connections. I've always thought it was amusing that most publishers are impressed by large numbers of social media connections when it's very likely that 90 per cent of those connections have neither the intent nor means to buy the book in question!

MASTERFUL INSIGHTS

Ask influential people to comment on your work and then reciprocate. That's another aspect of 'the chain reaction of attraction'.

Have a bit of patience and instead of spamming, invest in engaging with the people you'd like to eventually do business with. People buy from people they know, like and trust so take the time to develop a relationship, deliver value through your content and allow for consideration before you try to offer your services.

Any kind of 'pitch' in and of itself shows that you are an amateur in what you do. Professionals don't engage in 'spray and pray' marketing and pitch tactics, they develop relationships and through conversations with buyers and potential buyers, when they identify needs, they offer to help. They don't blindly do this with every person who says yes to a LinkedIn connection request any more than they would with a stranger on the bus. These are humans you're interacting with, not slot machines.

If anyone talks to you about 'elevator pitches', run from the room. They went out with poodle skirts and bell bottoms.

Your reputation is core to your brand. If you want to build a strong reputation, you can do this through the relationships you have built, the results you've helped others attain and the body of work you create. Your marketing is an extension of your reputation, so don't abdicate responsibility for your brand to someone else. Someone I know once called a professional author and speaker out for stealing other people's content from their websites and sharing it as his own. When confronted, this individual claimed he had no idea this was happening, he had hired someone to manage his marketing.

While it's fine to hire someone to manage your marketing, you're still responsible for how you are portrayed. (Think about the 'spam tag' example above.) You must inspect what you expect and ensure that you're managing your reputation accordingly. Regardless of whether this individual knew or not, he was responsible and by the time this was uncovered, due to the wide range of copying that had taken place, it was too late to remove the black mark from his reputation. Good news travels at the speed of sound in a socially connected digital world, but bad news travels at the speed of light.

Best practices for list-building are quite simple — offer value that people want to receive. Let them enter their

own email address and make it easy for them to unsub-
scribe. If you want people to stay on your mailing list,
treat them with the respect they deserve and show up
regularly with Masterful Marketing materials that make
a difference (such as models, checklists, language, visuals,
and so forth).

3

ALL YOU NEED TO DO IS CARE

WHY RECIPROCITY RULES

Most people think that they need to protect what they know and share only the bare minimum because they buy into the old metaphor, 'Why buy a cow when you can get the milk for free?' This old adage has changed – now you give away the cow and people will buy the milk from you for a lifetime. When you hold back what is valuable for others, you are acting from a place of scarcity. When you come from a place of abundance and share openly, the law of reciprocity kicks in and you attract greater opportunity into your life and business.

Alan has written over 60 books and they're in 15 languages. We're writing this one together. It's never dawned on us that these endeavours are anything but marketing channels for our services.

MASTERFUL INSIGHTS

No one ever learned to ride a bike or ski down a slope by reading a book.

Books create awareness, training can transfer skills, but only participation can create application. That's why medical students study, observe, practice under supervision, and then apply individually.

Providing your expertise for free simply whets people's appetites and prompts them to want more. Learning is not implementation. View it this way:

- Writing creates awareness and can transfer a few skills, but not complex ones;
- Speaking (including training) can transfer significant skills, though not pragmatically apply them;
- Consulting and advising transfer skills to pragmatic applications with oversight and feedback.

When I learned to scuba dive, I read up on the basics, the equipment and safety needs. I then attended classes and practised in a pool how to descend and ascend, check equipment and so forth. But then I went with my instructor and submerged 40 feet below the surface, where I could apply my skills and obtain real-time feedback from the instructor (hand signals can work wonders).

We live in a DIY, DWM and D4M world. DIYs are 'do it yourself' people: they will extract as much information as possible from your expertise and try to do it on their own. DWMs are 'do it with me' people: they want someone to guide them along the way, or hold them accountable for implementing the expertise. These people are relational in nature and when they have a trusted relationship with you, they will keep coming back over and over again because your expertise really helps them progress. Then there are D4Ms: they want you to do it for them. They have no interest in applying the expertise; they want an expert to do the implementation work, manage the process and customize the project specifically for them. These are high-end buyers who are busy and while they value your expertise, it is only the first step to engaging them as buyers. Your capacity to provide the additional service that does the work for them makes them an even higher value buyer.

In our experience we have found that there are significantly more DWMs and D4Ms than there are DIYs. (Note that in teaching hospitals, students watch a procedure, then do it with supervision, then do it themselves.)

Masterful Marketing is about recognizing with whom you are dealing. And the key to D4Ms is that the work they don't want to do needs to be shifted to their people, not to you. Otherwise, you're becoming a de facto employee and creating outrageous labour intensity for yourself.

When you give away your expertise, you also control your expert positioning. The more you give away, the bigger an impact and impression you make on other people. Your expertise becomes your body of work. Think of every piece of expertise you give away as a piece of paper. Over time, you keep adding papers to the pile and over time, this pile becomes your body of work. You, as an expert, stand on top of the pile of work, therefore the more expertise you give away, the taller your body of work becomes, and the higher you are positioned in your field of expertise. Of course, you'll have far more substance than paper!

One of the hallmarks of brilliant marketers is that they are generous. Thought leaders are generous: they readily share information, ideas and resources because they know in so doing they make themselves even more valuable. This is the reciprocity we speak of: The more you give, the more you get. People respond well to generosity, not so much to constant demands for money. That's why the best restaurant managers or bartenders will occasionally offer you a drink or even a free meal.

Reciprocity is amplified in four ways when giving away your expertise is at the core of what you do:

1 Retention of valued buyers: you attract and retain the best buyers based on your expertise and your ability to do what you say you can do.
2 Expansion of business: when your buyers experience your expertise, it becomes easy for you to

expand the amount of business you do with them and dramatically increase the lifetime value of your buyer.

3 Referral business: when your buyers are happy with your business, they refer their friends and colleagues to you. Not only do they refer, they endorse and recommend you based on their real-life experience.

4 Reputation enhancement: when you get to a point where you are able to retain your valued buyers, expand the business you do with them and receive regular referral business, your reputation is elevated by others in ways you could never do alone.

There is an old saying that charity should never be measured by how much one gives, but rather by how much one has left after having given. That's about money, which is a finite resource. But when we talk about expertise and talent, these are infinitely renewable resources and we can give as much as we like.

Counterintuitively, the more you give away, the more people are willing to pay. And while you might find a professional 'taker' at times who simply consumes, that person is the exception. Most people believe they get what they pay for, as we've previously demonstrated.

BUYERS LOVE TO BUY, BUT HATE TO BE SOLD

Today's most insidious snake oil sales people slither through LinkedIn. The minute you accept a connection request, you're likely to receive a message with the pitch of the day from one of these people, selling you products and services you have no need for all in the attempt to make a buck. These are the people who are only in it to make money. Transactionally focused, their hit rate is low and their rejection rate is high. They are emotionally desensitized from the way people respond to them, but it is the only way they know how to potentially win.

They don't care about the person or the relationship. I can buy and sell all of them ten times over, but they insist that they can help me market better, raise my fees, 'upsell'. They seek to make money at all costs, forget about relationships, trust and adding value. This 'spray and pray' recipe is guaranteed to ruin your reputation and lets everyone know you're desperate for your next sale.

There are so many people who have fallen into this twenty-first-century version of cold calling that those who really do create value and have a desire to help will stand out. The future is about enabling the buyer to buy, since they love to buy – that's why we call them 'buyers'! Pursuing people on social media whom you ostensibly want to join, or befriend, or follow, or link with, and then offering some deal to them is the modern, electronic 'bait and switch'. People are often fixated on increasing their social media connections – and figuring out why is the subject for a psychology book, because you can't pay the mortgage with 'likes' – so they are tempted to link with strangers. Admit it, you've often accepted invitations from people who are completely unknown to you.

Once you've taken the 'bait' the switch comes, which is the offer of some irresistible deal, which assumes:

- You're damaged or broken;
- You're not as successful as the person making the offer;
- You're willing to accept advice from unknown people;
- You're naïve.

MASTERFUL INSIGHTS

Buyers can reach their own 'close'. Trying too hard only increases your cost of acquisition – simple is best.

Buyers love to buy and they prefer to close themselves. The buyer's journey is no longer in your hands. Today's buyers are already on their own journey and they have pretty much decided what they are buying before they even make contact.

To think that you can orchestrate some type of journey to change this is ludicrous. The way people buy has changed and it requires you to change too. This is why the focus on sharing your expertise and adding value is so important. Your buyer will make their own emotional decision to buy when they are ready, not when you logically decide they should.

CASE STUDY

Friday morning, I woke up to a listing on the real estate website for a home in the mountains. We had been looking at mountain properties for some time, hoping to buy a cottage get-away, when this listing intercepted my morning coffee. This was no regular cottage, this was a beautiful townhome nestled in the mountains with a 'million-dollar' unobstructed view of the biggest mountain you've ever seen — and close to a million-dollar price tag.

We texted our estate agent instantly — the one we know, like and trust, who did nothing to help us find this listing (because we are in control of our own buyer's journey) — and before lunch that day, we had made an $855K cash offer on the property. By dinner, we were informed that there were multiple offers and the sellers wouldn't decide until Sunday evening at 6 p.m.

By noon on Saturday, we had prepared a second offer, no conditions and above asking price without having stepped foot onto the property. Sadly, we were outbid by $20,000 and didn't get the property — which is neither here nor there — and you should know the outcome: this entire journey symbolizes what today's buyers are like. When they see something they want, they act. They act from a place of emotion and will do things that defy logic to have what they want to buy.

Your expertise has to be what *intercepts* them on their journey and causes them to want to act at a time also favourable to you. When you provide value that is that appreciated, your buyers will move mountains to do business with you.

My tax firm routinely sends me videos and articles about subjects which might be important, from tax changes to loan options, and from investment rules to record keeping suggestions. They realize not every subject is appropriate for every client, but they trust that some are, and they're acting with the knowledge that all of us are on our journeys and they have to remain on our radar screens.

A brand is how people think of you when you're not around. Most of us automatically think of the right medical professional or dry cleaner or auto dealership, or art gallery based on a successful experience from our past. But when we can't, we ask someone we trust. You need to build your brand for both the initial thought and the person who has asked for a recommendation.

ALL YOU NEED TO DO IS CARE: CREATE, ATTRACT, RETAIN AND EXPAND

The CARE method is a simple and repeatable way to demonstrate Masterful Marketing. But simple does not mean that it is easy. This method requires you to continuously consider how to add value, how to better serve your ideal buyers, how to keep them interested in your work and how to be so masterful that they can't help but tell others about you.

The creation of value-based marketing is rooted in content creation. 'Content' is how you market to today's browsers and how you gain their interest in what product or service you offer. Content creation can take on a variety of formats, from written to audio, to video, and even textual visuals. When you care about your work and the people you serve, you will create value-based marketing on a regular basis. You will have to share your knowledge and expertise at minimum once a week.

When you create value-based marketing, it is crucial that you know who you are creating this marketing for. This requires a comprehensive understanding of who your buyers are, what their challenges are, the questions they have and their greatest aspirations for success. When you create for these people, instead of creating without intention, people start to feel like you understand them, their challenges and desires, and that they can trust you. You retain the interest of browsers and attract them as buyers in two ways: consistency and credibility. This means that you are consistent in the creation of value and the expert advice that makes an impact. When your knowledge is put into practice by others, they get results. This happens through their consumption of content and through your products and services.

MASTERFUL INSIGHTS

You listen to your ideal buyer, create appropriate content, which that buyer 'consumes' and which creates trust and credibility in your value.

When you do this well, and you do it repeatedly, people continue to do business with you. It's not unusual for either of us to have clients who have done business with us for a decade or more. When you retain your buyers, and continue to deliver value, they become raving fans of you and your work. They will refer you to people in their network and endorse your work. They will also provide you with written and video testimonials that you can use to validate the work you do and demonstrate to others the value you provide.

When it comes to asking for recommendations, be skilful in how to do this. We receive regular asks via LinkedIn from people we have never hired before, or from people whom we have done business with, but years later. The best time to ask for a recommendation is when someone tells you about the results they have experienced because of the work they did with you. When you ask for a recommendation, be specific about what you want them to say and always make it about them and how their recommendation can help other people who have the same challenges see what is possible. If you ask for a vague recommendation, you'll get that, or you won't get one at all.

If you ask and reference something specific that they have said to you, that is likely what you'll get back. Thus, CARE is about the reciprocity of identifying the ideal client, creating relevant and unique value, converting and sustaining their business and developing referrals and recommendations.

A sale has three aspects:

1 The immediate business.
2 Expansion business.
3 Referral business.

Too many of us leave one or even two of these routes 'on the table'. If you don't 'cash in' to the extent of, say, $100,000 a year, that's a half million in bottom-line business you will have sacrificed with no hope of ever reclaiming it. In ten years, it's a million.

We call this 'thinking of the fourth sale first'.

Before we close this section, let's deal with the mindset required to create these important traits and behaviours:

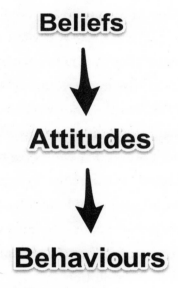

FIGURE 3.1   Beliefs to Behaviours

The mindset issue here is our beliefs. In the CARE process we have to believe that we are helping our client or prospect. We believe that we can help them and we believe it's a 'good deal' for them and for us — dramatic results in return for equitable compensation.

Those beliefs create attitudes. For example, I have to approach this person in order to help them, or only by asking for referrals will I be able to help others. Our attitudes are then manifest in our behaviours: we ask for referrals, we ask for appointments, we tell prospects that we're confident we can help them. Those behaviours 'inform' others about who we are. Thus, a mindset becomes 'visible' and effectively influences those around us.

ACHIEVING RESULTS INSTEAD OF CHASING MONEY

It's not what we do that matters, it's what we *create*. No one wants a drill unless they need a hole. No one wants better employee communications unless they create more business and lower costs. What we create is what improves the client's condition. We do that in return for equitable compensation. (That's why billing by a time period is unethical — as well as low-profit — because the client is best served by a rapid resolution but the consultant only makes money through a slow resolution.)[*]

We don't want to 'chase money' as though we're dogs chasing cars. The question arises about what the dog would do if it actually caught the car and whether money is

---

[*]See *Value Based Fees*, third edition, Alan Weiss (Wiley, 2021)

what you're after. Or are you pursuing a better life, more security, philanthropy and health? Wealth is discretionary time – the ability to go where you want, when you want. Ironically, the blind pursuit of money often erodes our wealth, since we spend *all* of our time trying to capture cash. Most of us who are entrepreneurs or boutique firm owners are refugees from larger companies and have gone out on our own to be independent. The problem is that many of us now have a tougher, more demanding, more miserable boss.

CASE STUDY

Jill was in a high-powered mastermind group. When it was her turn to discuss a challenge, she explained that she was in the midst of a very successful client project but there was no need to expand this particular project and there was a clear ending date.

She had learned that the client had freed up substantial funds for further investment and wondered how she might approach the client to become involved in this new 'windfall'. Jill was asked how much additional money was available and she said $400,000.

The group fell silent, then the facilitator said, 'Jill, my guess is that you're trying to figure out how to "capture" that entire $400,000. Am I right?'

'Well, yes,' she admitted sheepishly.

'My suggestion,' he said, 'is to offer to become a trusted advisor on as many issues as you have competency to deal with for your buyer on a retainer basis for the next year. That might amount to $150,000–$200,000. Don't be greedy. Ask where you can really help, not how much you can grab. If you do a great job over that year, there will be more business after that.'

And that's exactly what she did.

One of the greatest problems with professionals in marketing is that they emphasize what they *do* instead of what they *create*. Here is a 'typical' past of a consultant:

Consultant's past
- Experiences
- Education
- Accomplishments
- Development
- Travels
- Work history
- Beliefs
- Victories/defeats
- Risks/adversity
- Experimentation

We all experience these issues to some extent and they serve, one hopes, to make us better and more successful. These we may consider as our 'credentials'. That's the past, here's how these are conveyed in the present. They represent our current methodology and technology. We can convey our expertise – our experiences – in a wide variety of ways depending on our flexibility and comfort:

Consultant's present
- Coaching
- Surveys
- Publishing
- Training
- Speaking
- Facilitation
- Advisory services
- Etc

These are interventions in the present. Here are the results we'll be creating for the future, however:

Client's future
- Higher productivity
- Lower attrition
- Higher morale
- Improved image
- Better performance

- Greater market share
- Greater profit
- More growth
- More innovation
- Problems solved
- Happier customers
- Superior service

These and other benefits represent what we create for the client. These are the reasons we're hired.

So be aware of two key marketing points:

1 We have the ability to have learned from our past and utilize our technology and approaches in the present to improve the client's future. Almost no other profession can do that outside of personal and professional services firms. We are constantly learning and improve the client's future, which enables us to learn still more and be even more valuable to the next client.

2 Never charge for the first two columns! Only assign fees to the results you create – the improved client condition – not your credentials or technology. The first two can easily be perceived as commodities, but by putting them together, you create unique value in what you create.

MASTERFUL INSIGHTS

'CARE' creates the reciprocity that continually adds to your experiences and technology, which results in more dramatic improvements for your clients — the last of which justifies your fees.

4

CREATION OF VALUE-BASED MARKETING

FORMATS AND FRAMEWORKS FOR CREATING CONTENT

There are multiple formats that you can use to create content. The most popular ones are written, video, audio or visual. Each of these formats can be modified in order to take on various formats. For example, a written blog can be read out loud and turned into an audio file that can be used on a podcast, or a snippet of audio can be used to create an audiogram. The most important thing for you to consider is that the content you create, regardless of format, is what draws people to you and your work. It is how people begin their journey as browsers to get to know, like and trust you before they become buyers. Thus, the creation of regular content and use of multiple formats allows you to reach a larger audience.

We've always suggested that people publish (text, audio, or video) in places their ideal clients read or visit. When asked how to find out what those places are, we reply, 'Ask your ideal clients!'

When it comes to choosing a format, start with what is most comfortable for you to share your expertise, combined with what ideal buyers are watching and reading, and create value for them. If you are a speaker, you may find recording video or audio easier to do than writing. If you prefer to write, start there and then create outlines that you can use from your writing later on to create videos or audio recordings. Don't feel as though you have to use every format at once. While use of all formats is a good idea, it is more important to pick one that you're great at using and be consistent in your delivery of new valuable information.

MASTERFUL INSIGHTS

Repetition and consistency are the keys to effectiveness and recognition in any medium and in any format. That's why you keep seeing the same advertising over and over again.

Here are some common definitions and explanations of formats used for content creation and some basic frameworks you can consider:

1 Written: Written formats are usually considered blogs, articles or resources on your website. The

format used is writing and these written posts should be optimized with images, strong headlines, keywords and links to other areas of your website and they should contain shared link images that ensure the content looks appealing when shared in other places. The optimal length of written content is in excess of 300 words. We would also strongly recommend e-Books when you're ready, perhaps 30–50 pages in length. These are ideal for short-term marketing and can be easily updated and kept contemporary.

2   Video: Video formats can be video that is recorded or video that is livestreamed. The key difference is a recorded video can be edited and professionally polished before it is viewed by others, whereas a livestream video occurs in real time. Best practice for both recording of video and livestream is to be conversational, use bullet point notes to keep you on track and appear professional. (Attend to hair, make-up, clothing with the help of a professional if needed. No one wants to watch someone in a T-shirt or with their hair in their eyes.) The benefit of a recorded video is that you have more control over the content you've created. The benefit of a livestream video is people can engage with you while you are live. Both formats can be hosted on

sites like YouTube, Facebook, Vimeo or LinkedIn and all formats can be embedded onto your website for viewing.

3 Audio: Audio formats are usually recorded for podcasting, which has gained tremendous popularity over the last few years. A podcast is usually hosted through a site like Libsyn and is then consumed through a podcasting platform like Apple Podcast, Google Podcast, Amazon and a host of others. Your podcast can also be embedded onto your website using an audio player and you can create a highly valuable and rich user experience through the use of additional resources, downloadable PDFs related to the show, show notes and transcripts which encourage listeners to visit your website. The length of your podcast is up to you — some people have short shows, up to 15 minutes in length, while the average podcast is usually 30–45 minutes in length. Both of us authors have a podcast — Alan's is called 'The Uncomfortable Truth' and Lisa's is called 'She Talks Business'. Garage Band and similar software is a good alternative for a do-it-yourself podcast, complete with licenses, music and sound effects.

4 Visual: Visual formats entail the use of infographics, process visuals and more recently, swipe-able

content. Visuals are usually used to depict a process, illustrate some type of journey or to showcase small, bite-sized pieces of data or content in a swipe-able format – think quotes that swipe or a carousel of content that you can consume visually. When using visuals, ensure they are professionally created, using tools like Photoshop or Canva, and have a specific purpose related to your business. Simple quote graphics with no real meaning or purpose are considered obsolete today.

Eat your leftovers. Imagine for a moment that you have created the most decadent Thanksgiving dinner in the history of humankind. You've worked tirelessly in the kitchen for hours to ensure your turkey is cooked to perfection. You've gone to every grocery store in the area to compile the finest ingredients for your dressing, you've made cranberry sauce from scratch, and the finest pumpkin pie anyone has ever tasted. Your gravy is thick and delicious and paired with creamy mashed potatoes. This meal is fit for royalty and you've spared no expense to get it this way.

You then sit down, serve yourself one portion and then throw the rest out. No leftover turkey sandwiches, no turkey soup, no stew and no reheated delicious dressing. This is what happens when you create content, use it once and promptly forget about it. It's like making a turkey dinner without ever eating any of the leftovers. The leftovers from a Thanksgiving dinner can last you and your family for a week in many cases. The leftovers from your content can last for years. When you create masterful content, it should be part of your marketing mix for the long run. Don't treat the marketing of your valuable content as though it only has a single use purpose. Instead consider how you can repurpose your best content into other formats so you can continue to share and add value for others for a significantly longer period of time.

'HOW CAN I USE THIS?' THINKING

One of the most masterful attributes of creating great content comes from paying attention to your surroundings, applying a bit of curiosity and asking yourself, 'How can I use this?' Every day you witness situations around you and happening to you through interactions with family, friends and clients. When you start to view things through the lens of learning a lesson that can be used to create value, the ease with which you can begin to create a volume of content that is widely relatable heightens. This does require semi-deep-thinking! One cannot become a thought leader with an absence of thought. You must pay attention to what is going on around you and see through the lens of curiosity, ways in which you can use your life experiences to add value for others.

Consider a situation with a client where something humorous, impactful or difficult occurs. How can you take the situation, create anonymity for the client where appropriate and turn the situation into a story that provides value for others? When you use real-life examples of things like this in your writing, it becomes more impactful and relatable for others. Stories, metaphors and examples involving real clients are masterful and valuable because they allow others to see you at work and because many clients have similar challenges, it allows for them to see how you might help them in the same situation.

CASE STUDY

I was working for a major utility and one day the CEO called me aside and said, 'Drop your current consulting projects and find out what happened to our call centre operation. We've begun getting complaints about abruptness and cut-offs about three weeks ago and it's getting worse.'

'What happened three weeks ago?'

'Nothing at all, no changes in management, staff or procedures.'

'Okay, I'll go upstairs and have a look.'

'They're not up there anymore, they're across the street now.'

'Let me guess, did that happen about three weeks ago?'

'Well, I think so, but that can't be relevant.'

When I walked into the new quarters, I was shocked to see everything in red — carpeting, cubicles and walls. These people were irate at 7 a.m. when they started and the mood carried through the next shift: they were staring at red all day.

I found the CEO in a meeting with his top people. 'I have your answer,' I said, 'just paint the place.'

'Paint it?!'

'Why did you paint it red, anyway?'

'We wanted to save money and had extra paint around that we use to mark dangerous structures. Your advice is simply to paint it?'

'Yup, that's why I earn the big bucks.'

And I went back to my regular assignment. (They bought new paint, a light blue, and the complaints subsided to 'normal' levels the week following the new colour.)

Consider a situation you might observe, as in the case study, that has nothing to do with you. While out on our boat, I witnessed another boater get stuck on a remote island because they were not paying attention to the tides. Not only did their boat get stuck in the sand, when another boater arrived on scene, they didn't ask for help, nor did they call Sea Tow to help them. Instead they chose to put up a bug net and remained stuck until the middle of the night when the tide came back in.

When I witnessed this happen, immediately I started to consider the way business owners fail to heed warning signs (tide going out), fail to ask for help when readily available and instead suffer by themselves. You have the capacity to witness situations like this around you every day and use them in some way to inspire writing that is of value.

The utility thought it could save money by using excess paint and wound up spending more money and alienating customers because they never thought about the repercussions of their decision.

MASTERFUL INSIGHTS

Take specific incidents and generalize them so that they're applicable to a wide variety of people and situations. This is how simple it is to create intellectual property and marketing allure.

Another way you can do this is in the media. There are situations that you're reading about that can be turned into content creation. One Saturday morning, while reading the *Wall Street Journal*, I read about how the TV personality and writer Martha Stewart has upped her game on Zoom. 'How can I use this?' kicked in and I was inspired to write a post about how my own clients could up their own Zoom game and used Martha Stewart as an example of someone who was choosing to adapt to changing times.

DONE IS BETTER THAN PERFECT ... WHEN YOU'RE 80 PER CENT READY, MOVE!

Your first is your worst and you'll never improve if you don't move. This applies to your first book, your first blog, your first video, your first podcast and, of course, your first kiss. Perfectionism, fear of not being good enough and fear of what others may think prevents many people from starting, finishing and publishing their work in this world.

Publishing that video, blog or podcast can feel daunting, overwhelming and scary because you're putting yourself 'out there' and when you do that, you're vulnerable to criticism. When you allow this to stop you, you're really focused on you instead of creating value for others. While you may be vulnerable to criticism, you're also capable of making an impact in someone else's life through the value you create. Commit to the act of creating value over every creation needing to be extremely high in value. You don't know what value means to someone else, but you do know that your own inner critic can prevent you from starting and finishing work.

THE LOBSTER PRINCIPLE

No one knows how long lobsters live or how big they can grow. There have been reports of 80-pound lobsters and 100-year-old lobsters (both, thankfully, returned to the sea). A lobster has an exoskeleton – a shell – which must be shed – moulted – in order for it to grow.

While waiting for a new shell to form, the lobster is vulnerable and must hide from predators. When it is continually successful, it's too tough for most predators to take on. Hence, vulnerability is essential to growth. So, too, with us humans. Except, no predators are stalking us.

Imagine if Babe Ruth had failed to swing at a ball, or Ronaldo missed a penalty, because they were worried that they wouldn't hit a home run or score a goal? Great athletes don't become great because every shot they take is perfect, they became great because of the volume of shots they take and that includes the number of times they missed. (Babe Ruth led the league in home runs and strikeouts.) When it comes to creating valuable content for others, the same rules apply.

Every piece you publish isn't going to be a home run and you'll never become exceptional at it at all if you don't keep doing it. You get good at something through practice and repetition, not through paralysis-by-analysis. Momentum loves speed and if you spend a disproportionate amount of time trying to get from 80 to 100 per cent, you're going to slow your own growth and ability to help others. When it's 80 per cent done, move! Don't stay stuck in perfectionism. You're not serving anyone when you keep the value you can create inside of you.

It was a Saturday afternoon when I emailed Alan and asked him if he'd consider writing this book with me. He replied within the hour and said, 'Send me the premise and the chapter breakdown by Monday.'

I had less than 48 hours to put together the outline for a book that mattered greatly to me and I did it. Over the course of a two-week period, together we refined the outline, wrote a book proposal and a sample chapter. It was done with speed and it wasn't done perfectly but here we are now, having written the book in less than three months, with a publishing contract, writing this book at a rapid rate together. Had we stayed stuck in perfectionism, one of two things would have happened — it would have taken forever to get this book completed, or the book would have died while still an idea.

When you get stuck in perfectionism, and you don't take rapid and regular action, that's what happens to your ideas. They die and when they die, they are of no use to anyone else and they fail to deliver any value. Your ideas are valuable so keep them alive and get them out of you and out into the world as quickly as you can.

MASTERFUL INSIGHTS

Perfectionism kills excellence.

Procrastination is the belief that critique for not moving at all will be less painful than the critique of the completed project or effort. It is fear-based and debilitating. The best way to conquer procrastination is to 'go public'. Proclaim to friends or colleagues whom you see often that you will lose the weight, clean out the garage, make the sale, write the article. They will then hold you accountable merely through constantly asking you about progress.

I've found that anything I write is better than I thought, so that I never self-edit (review prior sentences) while writing, wondering if I could do it any better. The question is pointless. Perhaps I could do it better, but would the extra effort make a real difference? The audience doesn't appreciate the extra 20 per cent invested in perfecting a speech, nor the reader in writing the book, nor the facilitator in conducting a meeting. (Are you wondering whether this paragraph could be better written? No, you're not, and neither am I. You can always have your finished work reviewed by someone you trust afterward, but not *during* the writing.)

It's been said that Proust often spent weeks on a single sentence in *Remembrance of Things Past (À La Recherche du Temps Perdu)*. I've read it and it's turgid to the point of unreadable.

PAY ATTENTION TO WHAT PEOPLE ARE ASKING YOU

Start listening with two sets of ears. Use one set to carefully listen for the questions that people are asking you that you can use for content creation and the other to resolve the issue you're being asked about. Get in the habit of writing down the questions you're being asked by others so that you can start to identify trends and opportunities for content creation and to apply responses more generically.

If you do any type of coaching, either individually or in groups, transcribe your sessions and carefully pull out the questions you are being asked. Look for ways to use those questions to create value for others. Recognize that most of your clients have similar challenges and problems and thus, they also have similar questions they are looking for answers to. Hence, a 'generic' creation of responses.

Questions are good for attracting inbound leads and play a key role in Search Engine Optimization (SEO). While this book is not about SEO, this one tip can help you attract significantly more traffic to your website. Consider your own habits when searching for the answer to a problem you have. When you go to Google, or whatever search engine you use, you don't type the solution to the problem you have into the search bar, you type in the question. You type in the question because if you knew the solution, you wouldn't be looking for this information!

The idea behind this is using questions in your content and in the titles of your content that are a match for what others are looking for. When you do this, the search engines query the internet and find you, making it easier for you to stand out from your competitors. When you fine-tune your listening and you start to write content that allows people to easily find answers to the questions you have through your website, you create your 'stranger zone', a much more welcoming and valuable place for browsers looking to become buyers.

> ## MASTERFUL INSIGHTS
>
> No one buys a drill because they need a drill. What they need is a hole. No one puts answers into Google, they ask questions, because what they're searching for is a solution. Make yourself the solution.

You can also use questions to frame case studies and actual examples of ways that you have helped your clients. This is valuable on two fronts: one, you get the added benefit of SEO optimization from use of a question, and you get the real-life perspective, versus information only by incorporating a real-life example. People search for answers to questions but they learn by seeing the application of the solution and this is illustrated well through story-telling (also known as 'war stories').

Know what your audience prefers to consume when it comes to content. When you are searching for the answer to a question, Google will serve up many formats for you to choose from. You'll see links on the main page and you'll also be able to access videos and books. Soon you'll be able to access podcasts, too. When you create content using questions, pay attention to what content gets the most views. Is it the long-form written blog post you created, or the video on YouTube that you recorded? While this is not a precise science, my research from surveying groups of clients has found that when men are looking for information, they tend to prefer to watch a video, while women prefer to read information. It's a good idea to ask your clients what type of content they prefer to consume in order to ensure that your content can add value in the right way.

CASE STUDY

Questions are always a sign of interest. My programs are all interactive and I welcome questions throughout. I would gladly do an entire morning devoted to solely answering questions.

A third party was hosting an event which featured me. The host had specifically stated that there would be a question period at the conclusion, but I knew that would leave only about five minutes and a lot of unfulfilled curiosity. So, I merely stopped 15 minutes into the hour and said, 'Are there any questions?' The host had to frantically unmute people and monitor the chatroom. (Of course, this is no big deal when the event is live!) I did the same thing three more times before concluding. I didn't finish all my material, but I did create a much more satisfied and happy audience.

What you want to avoid is the absence of questions, which is a manifestation of apathy.

The other way questions can benefit you beyond ideas for content creation is through ideas you can monetize. Alan is known for regularly writing down ideas that come to him during conversations with clients that combine a question with a 'How can I use this?' mentality that suddenly becomes a program people are investing in. People learn in various ways and many want to be able to take the next step with you to get their questions answered in a deeper manner through private coaching, an online program or an in-person event. When you become masterful at listening to questions and grouping them together in a way that adds even more value, you can easily turn those questions into a highly valuable program that you can monetize and help others.

Let's move now to determining the right audience, the ideal buyer and how best to invest your marketing time, energy and talent.

5

ATTRACT THE RIGHT AUDIENCE

WHO IS YOUR CURRENT BEST BUYER AND WHO IS YOUR FUTURE BUYER?
The Masters Tournament is for people who like golf. Frank's RedHot website is for people who want to make their food spicy. James Patterson is for people who like to read mystery thrillers. Alan Weiss is for people who want to be great at consulting. So, who are you for and does your buyer know?

When it comes to Masterful Marketing, you cannot be masterful and attract the right audience if you do not know who your 'ideal' buyer is. It is the rare exception when people spend enough time clarifying who their current and future ideal buyer is – and they might be different people.

You cannot do this if you're chasing money, you can only do this if you truly care about your buyer, the issues they have and your role in helping to resolve them. When you think that everyone can be your buyer, you fail to isolate who is the best buyer for you and you end up spending time, money, energy and effort on things that are not necessary in your business. You may think all food is on your diet but some people can't tolerate the Japanese delicacy sea urchins, or rattlesnake or calf's brains. (Yes, they're all on some people's diets.)

Why does this matter? Because you cannot create Masterful Marketing when you are creating marketing for everyone. Consider this: have you ever gone to a high-end steakhouse like Capital Grill that also serves a vegan menu along with sushi and Indian food? Chances are you have not because a high-end steakhouse knows who their best buyer is and it's not someone who is a vegan. They will accommodate fish and vegetarian requests because these people might accompany their best customers.

When it comes to the attraction of the right audience, you do your buyer a disservice when you're not clear on who you are there for. If you are a leadership expert, trying to create content for stay-at-home mums doesn't make sense, even though some of your leaders might be mums who work from home. A high-end steakhouse has mastered both the category and brand of what they offer. Their category is a steakhouse, their brand is high-end. They are not trying to be a casual restaurant; instead, they cater to a market that wants surf and turf, white tablecloths, a nice bottle of cabernet, great service and exceptionally clean toilets.

There is nothing wrong with casual restaurants, they know what category they serve, too, and they also know what their brand is and who their best buyer is. There is a distinction in the quality of food, service and price points between these two restaurants. When you mix up your category and brand, and you can't get clear on who your buyer really is, you confuse people. And when you confuse a browser, you usually lose a potential buyer.

CASE STUDY

Many years ago, Mercedes sold only high-end, luxury automobiles. They then 'merged' (actually bought) Chrysler in 1998, which was a disaster, and subsequently divested. After that they went 'downmarket' and started producing far more inexpensive cars. Today, you can buy a Mercedes for as little as $30,000 or as much as $200,000. One problem is that too many of them look alike, removing the ego status of having the top of the line. But the other is that they're all serviced at the same place and quality of the vaunted Mercedes service department has plummeted in terms of speed, responsiveness and even quality.

Mercedes has lost sight of its ideal buyer and has lost the top-end of that market to Bentley and Aston Martin.

Where should you start? Start by looking at the buyers you have right now. Make a list of your buyers and write down why they engaged your services to begin with, what challenge or issue did they have and how did you help them. Next, make a list of how they found you – was it through a referral, an event, your book or your network? What do each of these buyers have in common?

As you can see in Figure 5.1, the bell curve has a third dimension. On the left are people who are apathetic. Then come 'pretenders' who talk a good game but are not buyers, merely gatekeepers. Then we have 'aspirants' in the middle,

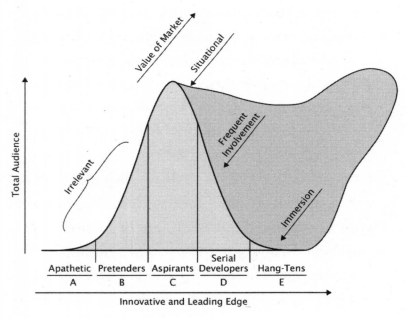

FIGURE 5.1 Finding the Ideal Buyer

who might be persuaded to 'come off the fence' and then 'serial developers', often called 'early adapters', who are eager to try new things. Finally, there are the 'hang-tens' (the most daring surf boarders who place their toes over the edge of the board for the greatest effects and thrills), who are the ones who will invest and take prudent risks. Your marketing to present and ideal customers should be these last two groups, with the power of depth – that third dimension.

You're better off marketing to 500 people in these two categories than 50,000 people in the other three. And you need to know who they are in the future.

Now look at that list and identify out of your entire list of buyers, who your best buyers are. Who invests the most, gets the best results and is the easiest to work with? Who provides the most expansion business and the most referral business? What do these people have in common? Once you look at your buyers through this lens, you start to see similarities and patterns that make it easier for you to create marketing that can help them, opportunities to expand future business with them and common trends in terms of how they find you. When you know these things, you can do more of what works (when it comes to marketing) and create exceptional value for your buyer because you really understand them.

MASTERFUL INSIGHTS

Do you provide continual business to the same providers (lawyers, accountants, repair shops, retail outlets) or have you changed providers? If the latter, figure out why you did it and why you became someone else's ideal future buyer.

When it comes to your future buyer, there are three things for you to consider:

- Where are you headed in terms of advancing your own expertise?
- Where are your best buyers headed next?
- What does the future version of those best buyers look like right now?

Think of your buyer's journey with you as leading you to the next iteration of your business. When you become a trusted advisor and service provider, your buyers will seek you out to continue to help them on their journey. Therefore, you should consider what comes next and proactively be considering how you can prepare them for what comes next in order to help them to get there. Without careful consideration of these things, you may miss key opportunities to create additional value for your buyers and retain them long term.

WHAT ARE THE BIGGEST CHALLENGES YOUR BUYERS ARE EXPERIENCING?

Your buyers' biggest challenges are your greatest source of ideas for marketing and the best way for you to add value. When you start to write and talk about your buyers' biggest challenges and showcase how to resolve them, you position yourself differently from other people. You start to build expertise and can become a trusted advisor to these buyers, but this is impossible to do without really identifying who this person is and how you can help them.

An exercise that can help you to do this is to make a list of all of your buyers. Next to each buyer's name, write down all the challenges you helped buyers resolve when you worked with them. As you start to do this for every buyer you've worked with, you will start to notice patterns and common areas where your buyers regularly have the same types of challenges. These patterns are your greatest source of information for creating content that is valuable and helpful not only to your current buyer, but to your future buyer too.

MASTERFUL INSIGHTS

Don't keep inventing the wheel. 'Routinize' what you do that will work for every client.

Another great way to identify challenges is to regularly survey your buyers and do your own research. A quick search on YouTube for your area of expertise will show you a curated list of videos that have topics related to your buyers' challenges. You can tell by the number of views on videos what resonates with people and then create your own content. Don't watch the videos – you do not want to steal someone else's thought leadership even by accident, but the titles they use can be a great source of content ideas for you to expand on in your own way, using your own intellectual property and subject matter expertise.

Hone your listening skills greatly, pay attention to the questions your leads and existing buyers ask you and get into the habit of writing these things down so you can use them in your writing, videos or podcasts. You may also want to ask people to 'tell you more' so that you can also identify what the next question is. Sometimes the first question is a surface-level question and when you invite people to share more, you get the deeper, more valuable question that they are looking for a solution to.

If you revisit Figure 1.1 (*see also* p. 7), this is a good point to realize that you can't be confined to what your clients need. In understanding what they say they 'want' you can figure out what they really need and/or will need in the future – what's labelled 'value distance' in the figure.

Responding to what people want makes you a commodity, which people tend to judge by price – the lower the better. But explaining that you're meeting a need that they didn't realize they had makes you a distinctive value provider without competition. Remember my car phone purchase? I didn't know I wanted a phone until the need (and ego need – first in New England) was made apparent.

The way you 'unearth' challenges in the present and future is to ask 'Why?' When people ask 'How?', which most people do, it drives the decision level downward to more specifics and into the weeds:

'I want to expand my business.'
'How?'
'By moving into new markets globally.'
'How?'
'With a greater internet presence allowing remote purchasing.'
'How?'
'By finding a technology company that can design that.'
'Can we qualify as a company to help you technologically?'

But now let's ask 'Why?' instead of 'How?':

'I want to expand my business.'

'Why?'

'Because I'll need more profits for our college education fund and our retirement planning.'

'Why?'

'Because I've determined that our current sales
growth won't support those needs in terms of my
compensation or the company's valuation.'

'Have you considered using your existing savings,
investments and assets in a different way to accomplish that instead of relying solely on business
growth in turbulent times?'

'What do you mean?'

'Let me explain how we can help you achieve your
goals without spending still more money in your
sales efforts.'

That's quite a different outcome, because when you ask
'How?' you go down the decision chain to tactics and tasks,
but when you ask 'Why?' you go up the decision chain to
strategy and goals. The latter are never commodities and
are highly more valuable.

Don't hesitate to explain future challenges your clients
and prospects are likely to face. We're all inured now to

disruption and volatility. We need to anticipate the challenges of tomorrow, not to merely avoid them, but to exploit them.

There are evergreen challenges:

- Profit
- Market share
- Revenue growth
- Attrition
- Expenses
- Succession
- Valuation
- Brand power
- Crisis management

And there are situational and 'new' challenges:

- Remote workers
- Technology
- Social justice
- Global rivals
- Supply chain
- Tax changes
- Regulatory
- Artificial intelligence
- Sales evangelism

All of these – and the many more they imply – are important in unearthing and providing resolutions to your future ideal client challenges.

WRITE FOR PEOPLE, OPTIMIZE FOR SEO

When people are searching for solutions, they typically go to Google. When you have a clearly defined list of every issue your best buyers have ever had, and you develop a body of work around those problems, you make it easy for Google to help people find you through your expertise. Pay close attention to what they type into Google and to the other queries that Google auto-populates for you when you type your initial query in. These additional common searches are great ways to expand your writing for the very things your buyers are looking for.

There are many things you should know about SEO, including keywords, meta descriptions, naming images, tags and overall performance of your website that will help people find you. While these things are important, you should learn and use SEO best practices to optimize your content and you should also write for people. When you create content with a specific buyer in mind, you make people feel like you're talking to them. When you create content and your primary focus is keyword stuffing, you lose the ability to resonate with people because what you have created doesn't sound natural. People buy from people they know, like and trust, which means you need to write for people, and specifically your ideal buyer first, and then optimize for SEO, not the other way around.

MASTERFUL INSIGHTS

SEO focus comes after people focus, not vice versa.

Two tips that can really help you when it comes to SEO and help your buyer when it comes to searching for you, are to frequently use questions in your writing and then answer the question. When you use questions to title your content, or as headlines, or sub headlines, you make it easy for your browser and potential future buyer to scan and find what they need. The second tip is to have a glossary of common terms somewhere on your website that can have great definitions and link out to content to support those terms.

The last few things that can help you optimize for SEO are simple and easy to do:

1. Ask your happy buyers to write you a Google review. When people search your name or company name, it is helpful for them to read what others say about you.
2. Claim your knowledge panel on Google. Don't know what a knowledge panel is? Here is Google's

definition: 'Knowledge panels are information boxes that appear on Google when you search for entities (people, places, organizations, things) that are in the Knowledge Graph. They are meant to help you get a quick snapshot of information on a topic based on Google's understanding of available content on the Web.' Many people have unclaimed knowledge panels and don't use this space to control what others see and read about you and your business.

3   If you have a physical location for your business, be sure to set your business up on Google too. Information on how to do this can be found at https://support.google.com/business/answer/2911778

SEO can be of help in marketing, but it's not the be-all and end-all, not a magic bullet. Reject the spammers and scammers who try to sell SEO optimization every day, usually from other countries. There's no guarantee that search engines will result in the ideal buyers finding you.

WRITE FOR THE BUYERS YOU WANT TO COME THROUGH THE FRONT DOOR, EVERYONE ELSE WILL COME THROUGH THE BACK OR SIDE DOOR

It is common to have different types of buyers. What is important when it comes to your marketing is that you are creating material to serve your best and ideal buyers. If, for example, your primary buyer is the CEO of a company, but sometimes HR is the department that reaches out to you, don't fall into the habit of creating marketing materials for the HR team. If you do this, you will lose the interest of the CEO, but if you write for the CEO, the HR team will still find value in what you do and continue to reach out to you to help other executives, including the CEO. Don't mistake someone who is doing the groundwork for your buyer as your buyer.

If you write for two types of buyer, perhaps you help executives and their teams, always try and take your writing up to the highest level. Create content that is directed at the senior level buyer and frame the material in a way that shows it is to help them help their team. While you may have expertise that is applicable to more than one person, remain steadfast in knowing who your primary and ideal buyer is. When you write for a far and wide audience, you run the risk of diluting your expertise and your message. Have clarity about who your buyers are and the problems they need help with, and your marketing becomes significantly easier to manage.

Refer back to Figure 5.1 (p. 80) to identify and reconfirm your ideal buyers. They are in the two categories on the far right. You're better off writing for 500 people there than 5,000 people elsewhere.

If you fire a rocket into space at a pre-determined destination and the aim is off by even a fraction of a per cent, the rocket may well end up in a completely different solar system. So picture your rocket aimed at your ideal clients but then someone comes along who can do business with you and pay your fee and you can help them. Why turn that down? You shouldn't. But that doesn't mean you change the direction of your trajectory. We call this 'side door' business. A prospect comes through the side door and you help them and they pay you. But this doesn't change the nature and direction of your business. It's a 'one-off'.

CASE STUDY

I was on the board of a shelter for female victims of domestic violence. *Pro bono*, I put the board through a strategy formulation process which worked very well. One of the board members was the local police chief.

'I love this process,' he said. 'Can you do this for my department?'

'Chief, I'd love to, but I'm afraid my *pro bono* dance card is filled.'

'Oh, I have a federal grant, I can pay whatever your regular fee may be.'

'Sit right down!' I said.

> I helped the department gain federal accreditation, which required a strategic framework. (It was odd doing a program with 11 armed men in the room!) However, I never kidded myself into thinking that police departments or non-profits were my ideal clients. This was a one-off.
>
> The trajectory of my rocket never changed.

We often believe that whoever compliments us or even pays us is an ideal client, but usually they are merely clients of convenience. If you would never market to such a client, don't reverse yourself because they've come to you. If you do so, your rocket is going to end up lost in space.

One of the forces that causes us to change our direction is the tendency to generalize a specific. That means we receive a single piece of feedback — good or bad — and we immediately universalize it. So someone in an airport bar, half-looped, while you're both waiting for a delayed departure, tells you that you should write a book about crowd dynamics in airport gate areas. You're a bit tipsy yourself and the more the two of you talk, the more it seems like a bestseller. You actually begin to tell others about this idea as though you have massive positive support and those who know better don't want to dissuade your passion and perhaps think they're wrong since you have such massive endorsement (the drunk in the St Louis Airport!).

Attracting the ideal audience is essential. Let's now turn to how to convert that audience into clients and how to sustain those clients.

6

RETAIN THEIR INTEREST AND ATTRACT THEIR BUSINESS

MIRACLES ARE INCREMENTAL

There is a funny meme shared on Reddit several years ago that comes to mind when we think about the marketing 'miracle' many people are looking for. Miracles require your participation.

> *Harry prays to God: Dear Lord, please make me win the lottery.*
>
> *The next day, Harry begs the Lord again: Please arrange it so I win the lottery, Lord!*
>
> *The next day, Harry again prays: Please, please, dear Lord, make me win the lottery!*
>
> *Suddenly he hears a voice from above: 'Harry, would you kindly go and buy a lottery ticket.'*

Masterful Marketing is a daily affair. You can't show up once and expect miracles from your marketing – that would be delusional, miracles are incremental. Trust, credibility and relationships are all built over multiple touchpoints, interactions and investments of time and energy over a period of time. When you C.A.R.E (*see* Chapter 3, pp. 48–52) and you are masterful in your marketing, you *want* to show up daily to contribute and add value for others. Mastery comes from repetition and a long-term commitment to doing something. You don't become masterful when you do something once, it takes commitment, repetition and time.

MASTERFUL INSIGHTS

When you're passionate, nothing is onerous. When you're indifferent, everything is a tough job. You had better become passionate about marketing so that you are able to help people, or look for another line of work – preferably solitary.

During a recent webinar for the Society for the Advancement of Consulting, the concept of showing up daily to add value as a way to strengthen your brand was discussed. I was challenged by one of the members as to whether it would work for his buyer. This individual wasn't convinced that their 'showing up' daily and providing value would make an impact – and it won't if you do it sporadically and for a short period of time.

It takes at least six to 12 months of consistency in this type of marketing effort from the start to develop authority and influence in your sphere of business and then ongoing effort is required to become a masterful marketer. When this individual was asked if he had ever committed to this practice consistently for a six- to 12-month period, he responded that he had not.

You can't expect miracles to happen while you're busy rationalizing why something won't work. After the session, another consultant wrote this:

Excellent session. Thanks.

I didn't want to interrupt your discussion with 'Rob' but you can quote my story which is this...

Six months ago, I'd have strongly doubted your opinion, re: posting every day.

For five months now, I've done just that — posted daily. In that time, I've obtained:

- *Two invitations to speak at events.*
- *One project because an old contact was reminded of what I did.*
- *A potential executive coaching project (three VPs) with another client. We had a meeting last Thursday.*

I can't 100 per cent prove causation, but I'm 99 per cent sure that the consistency strategy you talk about makes the difference.

The key to traditional advertising has always been about frequency and consistency. That is, you repeat the same message over and over before it begins to 'penetrate' all the surrounding noise and distraction. I've heard people remark, 'They've run the exact same ad three times during this show,' which demonstrates that they're at least talking about the ad.

Too many people believe that marketing is a dramatic 'one-shot' effort. We all remember Apple's grand challenge to IBM (aka 'Big Brother') in that iconic Super Bowl commercial. But that is the rare – and hugely expensive – exception which simply proves our rule: You have to stay on ideal buyers' radar screens.

Branding represents a 'uniform expression of quality' to the academics, but to us it's simply – and far more importantly – how people think of you when you're not around. (Note: you'll read *that* message more than once in this book.) People used to thrust business cards at me, as if I'd seriously buy a mobile phone or hire an accountant or recommend a speaker because they've given me a business card. When I walked out of the meeting, I dumped a dozen cards into the litter bin. Why would I care about a stranger who apparently knows zero about marketing?

There is absolutely no one who rummages through a desk drawer to review scores of business cards retained from chance meetings and kept in order with a rubber band to find a professional to mow the lawn, much less buy a product or procure a high-priced service. In the 'old days' no one used the vaunted Yellow Pages to find a heart surgeon to call and today, no one surfs the Web using Google to find an outstanding real estate lawyer.

Instead we ask for suggestions from trusted colleagues. We recall constant value that has been provided by others. Remember the banks and dentists and repair people who would send you a small calendar every year, pre-smart-phones, so you'd record your meetings and appointments in there and see their names every time? That was a primi-tive form of firms today sending you free newsletters and insights by email (or even hard copy). The idea is to keep your name in front of the buyer, consistently and frequently, so that when the appropriate need arises, voilà! You're thought of.

Here's still another technique …

PAY ATTENTION TO WORLD EVENTS AND INJECT YOURSELF INTO CONVERSATIONS

If you want to capture someone's interest, it helps if you're interesting and have interesting things to say yourself! When you become an object of interest, and regularly contribute content and commentary that is stimulating, valuable and insightful, people start to pay attention to you and your work. Even if they have never met you, they start to develop a perceived relationship with you because of the information they have consumed and the interactions they have had with you.

When you attend a networking event, make every effort to connect with other people. You don't show up and sit in a corner by yourself and try to avoid talking to people (unless you're Alan, because people come to him!). You try to be interesting, build rapport and converse with people.

The same is true when it comes to marketing your business online. You need to make an effort on social media, on your blog and through your email communications to be interesting, helpful and establish relationships with people. Relationships are not B2B or B2C (business to business, or business to consumer), they are people to people and people make buying decisions. You cannot be masterful in your marketing and influence others without engaging with people.

MASTERFUL INSIGHTS

There is a tropism that is created by being an 'object of interest'. Think about people who enter a room and immediately attract others. This applies both in person and on the internet.

One of the ways you can become interesting, above and beyond your subject matter expertise, is to pay attention to world events, sports and pop culture and have an opinion on these things. A masterful marketer can synthesize and contextualize what is happening in the world in relation to their subject matter expertise. When you do this regularly, you demonstrate the depth and breadth of your value to others. You show that you are worldly and have vast knowledge on many topics and this in itself is interesting. When you do this, be mindful of polarizing conversations that are not relevant to your work, unless you really don't care if you alienate your buyer.

The goal is to show up in a way that resonates or provokes interest with those you want to do business with, even if you're being contrarian. It's not to engage in or attract online trolls and inappropriate bickering or to come across as proselytizing.

CASE STUDY

I was working with a woman who is a trained classical pianist. Her 'day job' is as a marketing consultant. I told her she was missing an excellent opportunity by not combining her vocation with her occupation.

'Do you expect me to play at the prospect's office?!' she asked.

I suggested she include a music theme on her site, in her speeches and in her collateral materials. For example, marketing must be in harmony with perceived needs, or even the best musical talents need a (marketing) conductor.

She did so, loved the combination, increased her passion and therefore grew her business.

You should also have a short list of keywords or hashtags related to your area of expertise that you follow. When you follow keywords related to a topic, you can insert yourself into conversations other people are having to add your perspective. Many of these conversations are taking place publicly on social media sites and on blogs and provide you with an opportunity to share your insights and be seen by others who are interested in this topic.

At the time of writing, there are over 3.6 million people who follow the hashtag #business on LinkedIn. When you follow hashtags related to your work and those you wish to engage with, you'll see public posts in your newsfeed that you can comment on and interact with. When people see your comments, it provides a one-click opportunity for them to view your LinkedIn profile and learn more about you — which is one reason why your LinkedIn profile and description of your services should also be interesting and engaging.

Some further ideas/musts:

- Read the *Wall Street Journal* daily, as in *every day*. I read it no matter where I am in the world, even if it's a couple of days late. You can read it online. It's one of the best-written newspapers in the world, covers the news objectively and honestly, and includes sections on the arts, sports and entertainment as well. I've often picked up a talking point with a client from that morning's *WSJ*.

- Use Google keywords to be informed of articles and announcements that are relevant. If we place '*Masterful Marketing*' on there, we'll learn daily if anyone is mentioning the book or the phrase, whether referring to Alan's work or anything else. You might place in words such as: innovation, technology, attrition, organization design and so forth.

- Don't take sides and ask yourself 'Why?' No matter what your personal beliefs, try to understand why people are reacting the way they are and how you can inform and help your client. And follow former US President Thomas Jefferson's advice: In matters of taste, swim with the tide; in matters of principle, stand like a rock. Help your clients to position themselves positively and ethically (their legal departments will look after legally, but not the rest).

SHOW, DON'T JUST TELL – PEOPLE BELIEVE ONLY WHAT THEY SEE

Not all of your clients want to be showcased in your marketing, but you can develop the skill of seeding without naming and sharing without breaching confidence.

As long as the basis of what you are sharing is true, it's okay to change a few details. For example, if one of us helped a client in healthcare with strategy today, we might say we helped a client in healthcare last week, instead of today, so that client doesn't feel like we are referring to them. In some cases, we'll say 'a client' and refrain from saying the specific industry, or whether they are a male or female to help them retain anonymity. A phrase such as, 'I was helping a major financial institution during the past year' is fine.

When your client kisses and tells, that changes the rules of engagement. When your clients speak publicly about you and the impact of your work, pay attention and share their success. The purpose of sharing isn't to shine the light on you (even though that might be what you want), it is to show what is possible for others and to celebrate what your client has attained.

MASTERFUL INSIGHTS

What we call 'war stories', whether specific or made generic, are key to creating emotional response from others and departing from the purely conceptual (and boring).

When demonstrating how you help people, keep these guidelines in mind:

- You can cite an organization as a client so long as that organization does not specifically prohibit it.
- You *cannot* use the client's logo or other artwork without their permission.
- You cannot cite the exact work you did or the names of people or quote people working for the client without permission. We suggest that such permission is always obtained in writing.
- A client is someone who pays you. Do not include *pro bono* examples or favours unless you stipulate that is the situation being cited. (We've seen speakers cite as their accomplishments the reading of prayers, eulogies and free sessions on social media platforms. All of that hurts more than helps, showing they don't have more substantive social proof to provide.)

CASE STUDY

Bill was the CEO of a large hospital. On every floor in every building there were framed printings of the organization's 'values', the fourth of which was 'We respect our employees.' Yet you could, metaphorically, see managers beating people in front of the signs, berating them, embarrassing them, showing disrespect for them. Bill wasn't blind to this, but he was astonished.

'How can this happen?' he asked. 'Why don't they practice our value statements?'

'Bill,' I said, 'do you think people believe what they read on the walls or what they see in the halls?'

There is a huge, cosmic difference between people who try to help you by saying, 'Let me tell you how I do it,' and those who say, 'Let me tell you how you can do it.' Most of the time, telling you how I do it can be meaningless because it's reliant on my talents, skills and passions, not yours. So, telling you to do what I've done – write 60 books that appear in 15 languages – is rather condescending and stupid, irrespective of whether you can walk over hot coals or not.

But telling you, 'If you're interested and have a flair, I can show you how *you* can write a book to market your business even if you've never written one before,' might be extremely useful. Of course, you'd have to have *seen* the books and the proof of my credibility, not just hear me talk about it. The internet has enough frauds claiming that they can help you in matters in which they themselves have never been successful to sink a battleship.

You might be skeptical, thinking that excellent marketing is about telling people things and appearing in certain venues, real and remote. A book, after all, is something they're reading. Evangelists, lauding your talents, are people they're hearing. But the real deal is *you*. People are influenced by what they see and we all only get one first impression. That old saw about books and covers is just a wish. People often *do* judge books by their covers, which is why publishers pay so much attention to them!

CASE STUDY

I worked with an insurance company's executive vice president of human resources. He told me that he knew for a fact that his staff were breaking the rules: charging lunches with each other but claiming they were with clients and taking time off for industry meetings that didn't really exist. He asked me to find out why.

I did so in two hours of interviewing. It turned out that the Vice President was entitled to fly first class but chose to fly coach, cash in the first-class tickets and pocket the difference. He bragged to everyone about this and his income 'boost'. When I told him that his people were simply emulating his own practices in 'working the system' he became furious.

'You're fired,' he yelled, 'I didn't hire you for you to tell me that I'm the problem!'

'Fine,' I said and turned to go.

'Wait!' he screamed, 'I paid your fee in advance!'

'What's your point?' I asked and walked out the door.

MAKE IT EASY FOR PEOPLE TO ENGAGE WITH YOU IN YOUR 'COMMUNITY'

There are several ways for you to build community, both within and outside of social media that will allow for people to easily engage with you. LinkedIn and Facebook groups are one way, so too are other online communities such as AlansForums.com (restricted to his clients), which can be set up using a variety of membership software programs.

When you think about your community, there are several layers. There are members of your community who are colleagues and trusted referral partners, there are people who consume and engage with your free content and there are buyers who invest in your programs and services. You should be mindful of how you distinctly engage with these individuals and the ways in which you build communities to allow for greater and greater levels of access to you and your work.

Community isn't static, it isn't limited to inside a group or forum, it extends to all interactions with you, online and in person. In some cases, communities are even formed around your work without you even knowing. A masterful marketer recognizes the power of community and will make it easy for people to engage with you and with each other. While your inclination might be to try and isolate and categorize different types of communities, this can be a mistake. Your community of buyers and non-buyers can greatly influence your next browser's buying decision by the way they interact with each other.

When it comes to community, there is a ceiling of trust that is typically not broken through until someone has met you in person (see, not read or hear). Each business is different as to what the monetary threshold is but if you do an analysis of your buyers, you should be able to see this easily. We've seen buyers who baulk at investing $10,000 prior to meeting us in person, quickly invest hundreds of thousands of dollars after one in-person interaction. This is the power of community – you can bring buyers and non-buyers together and your buyers will help your non-buyers (or lower-value buyers) break through the ceiling of trust with relative ease.

While we have been using online technology for a number of years now, trust is strengthened through in-person interactions and the more people know, like and trust you, the more they are willing to invest.

You cannot automate your communities. While there are many tools and technologies that will allow you to automate posts or direct messages on social media, and others that allow you to automate emails, auto responders and text messaging, you cannot and should not try to automate connection. Automation should be used to make access to information easier for your buyers and browsers, it should never be used to abdicate your responsibility for connecting and establishing relationship. While you may be tempted to use tools to reduce time and effort, be

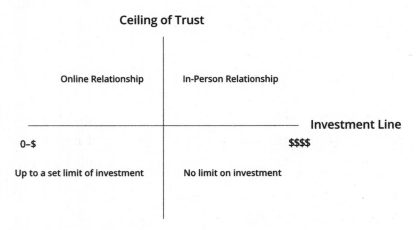

FIGURE 6.1 Trust and Investment

mindful of the potential cost of a relationship when automation goes wrong.

MASTERFUL INSIGHTS

The greatest value of community is in connecting
people who would otherwise not know each other
but profit greatly from knowing each other. As you
read this, that phenomenon is happening globally on
AlansForums.com.

One of the greatest benefits to your bottom line in building
communities is Invitation Marketing, an effortless way to
sell your ideas without doing any work! When you have a
strong community, you can ask them if they are interested
in something before you go through the work of setting
up sales pages and marketing materials (and even creating
content or finding a venue). A community that is invested
in your work, which engages with you regularly, will be
responsive and will shortcut many of your marketing efforts
by telling you which ideas resonate with them or not.

When you make it easy for people to engage, they are
more subject to the evangelism of others and more able
to 'see' you and the value you provide first-hand. They can
also experience a momentum to move towards more and
more valuable offerings at higher and higher prices and
fees. Here's what we mean in the Accelerant Curve:®

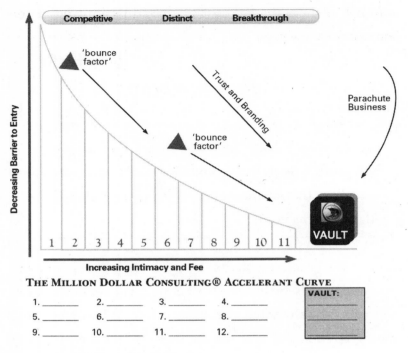

FIGURE 6.2 The Accelerant Curve

Counterintuitively, as the movement is to the right your fees increase while your labour decreases! This culminates in your personal 'vault', where there are offerings of value that only you provide (e.g. Alan's Million-Dollar Consulting® College or Lisa's Thought Readers Book Club). 'Bounce factors' include the community's evangelists, who prompt people along with their own 'war stories'. Once your brand is strong enough, 'parachute business' descends directly into your vault and doesn't have to enter on the left.

You'll note at the top of the chart that moving in this direction requires a change from competitive offerings to distinctive offerings and, finally, to breakthrough offerings. Your brand and trust in you encourages people to your community but also propels them into the best possible relationships.

Now let's turn to some best practices and find out how to improve the bad practices.

7

EXPAND YOUR REACH THROUGH RECOMMENDATIONS AND REFERRALS

WRITE SOMETHING WORTH SHARING

Stop asking people to 'share this post' in the description of what you post on social media. Instead, write something so good it makes other people look good when they share it. Back in 2007, when the share button was a novelty, asking someone to share worked because it was new and exciting for everyone. Today, asking people to share comes across as a bit desperate. Be confident and competent enough to write content that is useful, valuable and helpful for others: you can't 'make' something go viral; it goes viral because it's good.

Calls to action matter, but the call to action to share is passé. Instead stretch your creativity and use language that engages others without the need to ask someone to do something. This can be done through the thoughtful use of questions, but remember, a question alone does not elevate your thought leadership.

Asking someone if they prefer chocolate or vanilla might elicit many responses but what does that do for your brand? Nothing. Sharing a story around the impact of COVID on entrepreneurship and asking people whether or not their business has been impacted by COVID makes sense if you are in the business of helping entrepreneurs in business and you're trying to assess the impact of COVID and gather information on other people's experience. When you take time to think about the appropriate way to get others to engage, it's a conversation, and when you start a conversation that matters to people, and is related to the work you do, you attract the visibility of both browsers and buyers, and show that you can facilitate valuable community conversations.

Poor example: Do you think your organization innovated consistently?

Better example: What's the best example of innovation you've experienced?

Great example: Here's my best innovation practice: give people the freedom to fail. There are three aspects to doing this successfully ...

Don't be afraid to share something you think people should have to pay to know. When you share content that is valuable enough for others to pay for, you automatically elicit shares and conversations around your work. Be confident and avoid a scarcity mentality when it comes to sharing information. Remember, information is only one part of the equation, people need help with insights related to information as well as implementation. Once they know you have the right information, then they can consider how your insights and ability to implement can help them.

MASTERFUL INSIGHTS

Counterintuitively, the more you charge for information, the more the buyer perceives its worth.

Vanity metrics don't pay your mortgage and they definitely don't earn compound interest in your bank account. Be more concerned about quality than quantity, with valuable content and conversation more important than the number of likes, comments, 'reactions' and shares. While these things are great for elevating your visibility, remember, the 'creeping factor' related to The Stranger Zone: People are too often consuming what you write without engaging with the content. Just because no one commented, doesn't mean you didn't make an impact. The absence of evidence is not evidence of absence.

And if you do want people to engage with your content, do the very thing you'd like others to do — engage with other people's content. Someone once expressed to us concern that if they shared content and no one engaged then it would make them look bad. We asked how often they engage with other people's content they read and value, and they said, 'Not very often,' and yet, they didn't think those people 'looked' bad. If you want people to engage with you, start by engaging with them and don't forget to respond once they do start to comment on what you share. Let them know you see what they wrote and be social, don't ignore them.

CASE STUDY

When I was fired from my corporate job and was trying to get established, before the age of the internet, I asked myself how I could stand out in a crowd of 250,000 or so consultants in the US. I decided to be 'the contrarian' (a sobriquet that remains with me 30 years later). I 'took on' the fanatic focus on quality at the time – quality circles, black belts in quality, lean and so forth, *ad nauseum*.

I wrote an article, 'Why Quality Isn't Worth It', for a Boston magazine, which accepted it. The reaction was quick and almost violent. The entire quality crowd wrote angry letters and there was a firestorm. I felt so bad that I called the editor to apologize.

'Kid,' he said, 'I'll give you $50 bucks a column, one a month.'

'But they hated it,' I said.

'Yes, but they *read* it,' he pointed out.

I wrote 72 columns over six years until the magazine was sold. The column was called *Revolutions*. I acquired a ton of business from them.

No one wants vanilla, they want irresistible flavours. Yet many people aren't bold enough to cause a stir. They stick their toes in the water instead of making waves. If you write something provocative, however, they're happy to share it and repeat it and cite you. They're joining the 'movement' but cannot be blamed as the 'originators'!

The value you create is often in possessing and sharing a different view and providing examples of why you're right and the prevailing view is not. You'll be pleasantly surprised by how many people out there rise to agree with you, people who didn't have the means or courage to write or speak those same truths.

Let's look at some ways to most easily 'share the wealth' of information.

USE HASHTAGS WISELY AND RESPOND TO COMMENTS REGULARLY

Hashtags (#) are a great way to follow conversations that are relevant to your industry and that matter to your buyer. You can learn a lot by following hashtags and seeing what other people are talking about, and on most social media channels, you can see the number of followers and or volume of use for hashtags. When you follow a hashtag, there are a number of benefits for you:

- You obtain visibility about what is being discussed in real time;
- You achieve insights and ideas on content you could create to add to the current discussion;
- You can increase your visibility and be seen by potential new buyers when you comment on other people's posts related to the hashtag;
- By commenting regularly on these topics, you stand out as a subject matter expert and object of interest.

Don't engage in hashtag spam. While it may seem logical to use a popular hashtag for every post, avoid doing this. You are better to have a smaller number of niche hashtags that you use, that are of interest to your browsers and buyers than you are to engage in what is called 'hashtag hijacking'. Hashtag hijacking is when you try to hijack the conversation around a hashtag for self-serving purposes. A great example would be using a hashtag for a natural disaster such as #HurricaneIrma to try and pitch your services to a larger audience. Years ago, retailers such as American Apparel faced a backlash from Twitter enthusiasts when they tried to take advantage of a natural disaster to promote a sale.

Another cardinal sin is to include someone else's name, who has a larger following, in your hashtag spam, even though that person has nothing to do with the subject and might not even know you. It's an effective way to create long-term animosity — that person will be notified about every post on the subject.

When you create a hashtag, be sure to read it with and without camel casing. Camel case is when you capitalize each word to make it stand out, such as #MasterfulMarketing. When you use camel case, it's easy to read the words but when you don't, other words can appear, such as was the case for Susan Boyle, the great singer, when her team used #susanalbumparty, which was really meant to be read #SusanAlbumParty!

Treat comments like conversation. Have you ever gone to a networking event and ignored the person speaking to you? Likely not, because that would be rude. The same is true when it comes to social media. Social media is essentially networking online and there is etiquette that can make you stand out from the rest in a positive way.

When you post something on social media, your intention is to start a conversation, hopefully with a buyer or a browser. When someone engages in that conversation, even if they are not an ideal buyer or browser, other people can still see how you respond. If you ignore the comments, you are essentially saying that what they have said doesn't matter to you.

MASTERFUL INSIGHTS

In social media conversation, observe the same etiquette you would if you were networking in person.

While some comments may not require a response, it is good etiquette at the very least to like the comment as a form of acknowledgement and, whenever possible, to respond with a comment of your own. As an aside, responding to comments should be done by you, personally. If you've hired a team to post content on social media for you, you cannot delegate relationship building – that still resides with you.

Comments and engaging with others should be rooted in integrity and that requires you to show up and participate. Years ago, while working with a shopping centre, our team was engaged in sharing content and responding to shoppers on behalf of the mall. Most of the people who followed that particular shopping centre knew who the marketing director was and thought that the comments were coming directly from her.

One day, I advised her not to be shocked if someone approached her at the centre and expected her to know who they were. The more engaged the community became, the more they felt like they knew this person! Sure enough, one day while grocery shopping someone approached her and asked her a question related to social media, and she was prepared with her response. Otherwise, it would have been a very awkward encounter that diminished trust with the centre. A shopping centre can delegate posting and comments to an outside party, but if your brand is a personal brand, or if the comments are related to a personal profile, it's in your own best interest to engage and interact with people yourself.

Don't overuse hashtags because they won't serve your purpose. People will 'wise-up' to the lack of quality and/ or relevancy and you could be reported for abuse.

CASE STUDY

I had a very fine client whom I helped significantly. Part of her marketing campaign for her professional speaking involved heavy social media promotion. She entrusted this to her technology firm.

I began to receive continual notices from LinkedIn about people commenting on a posting that mentioned me. This occurred daily, several times. I tracked down the post and it was from this client. At first, I couldn't find my name mentioned anywhere in the post or responses. But then I noticed it, amid three dozen names with hashtags. Her team had simply included all the people she knew who might be a 'draw' and included them without permission. When I informed her, she was mortified and had the posting changed, but to many people who didn't bother to contact her that bad decision appeared to be hers.

So, ask yourself the Kantian Categorical Imperative: What if everyone did that?

What does all this work on social media and with hashtags get you? It gets you referrals.

EARN THE RIGHT TO ASK FOR RECOMMENDATIONS AND REFERRALS

Social proof is a powerful way for you to turn browsers into buyers. Word-of-mouth marketing is now *world*-of-mouth and provides many opportunities for business owners — when done well.

Many online marketers participate in proverbial 'dog and pony shows', where they parade their clients around online and get them to share success stories in an effort to pitch and close services. It comes across as very choreographed and self-serving, and is not the best way to approach developing social proof.

Social proof is a psychological and social phenomenon wherein people copy the actions of others in an attempt to undertake behaviour in a given situation. The term was coined by Robert Cialdini in his 1984 book *Influence: The*

Psychology of Persuasion (HarperCollins, 1984), and the concept is also known as informational social influence.

When it comes to social proof, you have to learn to listen and ask at the right time. For example, a client once told me during a strategy session that he wished he had met me sooner; it would have saved a lot of time and money and helped the company get ahead faster. A week later, I asked for a recommendation on LinkedIn and referenced specifically what was said to me during the strategy session and how such a recommendation would help other people who were wondering if there were value in doing this work.

MASTERFUL INSIGHTS

The company obliged immediately. The time to ask for a recommendation is when your client is telling you that your work is great.

Don't treat recommendations as a monthly 'to-do' item. Instead listen regularly to what your clients say and use their words in a timely fashion when you ask for a recommendation. When you ask for a recommendation on LinkedIn, there is a default message that says, 'Hi (name), could you write me a recommendation?' This is the most *ineffective* way to ask for a recommendation because the person you're asking doesn't know how to help you. What's even worse is when someone who has never done business with you asks you to do this! So ask for recommendations with intention *and* do so once you've earned the right to ask. You earn the right to ask when you've delivered value and your client has told you as much.

Recommendations on LinkedIn are public pieces of content and that means you can link to them from your website. When someone writes a recommendation for you, it shows up on your LinkedIn profile for anyone to see unless the person withdraws it. For these reasons, I recommend using LinkedIn as the vehicle to ask for a recommendation and then using that same recommendation as a testimonial on your website with a link back to your LinkedIn profile, where browsers can view more of them. However, the best requests for referrals and recommendations are truly inter-personal, high touch, not high-tech. You want to personally ask your client or key contact. Listen carefully: I've found that *most* people actually fear asking for referrals because they are afraid of being rejected! That's right, afraid to ask a client who loves their work for a referral or recommendation.

Why is this? Here is a list of possible reasons:

- Fear of appearing too aggressive;
- Fear that they're wrong in assessing the client's happiness;
- Insufficient hard evidence that their help actually created improvement;

- Thinking it's 'inappropriate' and 'unprofessional';
- Intimidation, seeing the buyer as a 'superior'.

Let me remind you that the real estate, insurance and auto industry sales are almost purely based on referral business. Referrals are zero-cost options to gain new business leads. They can fill our 'pipeline' continually and with minimal effort.

The key to referrals is that you ask either for a name or a position:

I would love an introduction to the CEO of your biggest supplier whom you cite as being very innovative in developing her people.

You've mentioned Harry Clark as your West Coast counterpart. Would you be willing to introduce me so that I can share with him what you and I have done together?

Never merely ask 'for names' because the people will respond that they'd like to think about it and get back to you. And never agree to 'provide some background material' because it's an excuse not to do anything and/or they'll just forward it as an 'FYI'.

Use this language for the prior requests:

It's inappropriate for me to expect you to do my marketing and you'll be asked questions that you won't be able to answer. All I'd like is a simple introduction or permission to use your name when I call them.

The language is as simple as that.

CASE STUDY

When I had just begun working for Prudential Life Insurance right out of undergraduate school and my wife worked as a teacher and we had practically no money, one day there was a knock on our apartment door.

The caller's name was Hal Mapes and his job as a Prudential agent was to sell insurance, which included selling to employees. I explained I had no money, but Hal asked how it would look if I were an employee without Prudential insurance. What were my chances for promotion?

So I bought the cheapest policy available — I think they threw me off a train when I died, somewhere in the countryside.

Then Hal said, 'Give me three names of people who also need insurance.'

'I don't know anyone,' I said.

He said, 'Sure you do. Your former classmates, your colleagues at work, people in this community, people with whom you play sports, just three names.'

Eventually, I came up with them.

Hal came back in six months to see if we needed more insurance. Had we begun a family as yet? Then he asked for three more names. We went through the same dance.

Six months after that, I thought I'd be defiant and so I told Hal very assertively that I had no names. He looked at my wife and said, 'Could I trouble you for another cup of coffee?' He wasn't leaving!

After that, I simply gave him three names every six months.

Do the math. Hal probably had about 200 clients when I met him and visiting each one every six months and asking for three names a visit would net him about 1,800 names. Let's say that 10 per cent agree to see him — 180 — and a third of them purchased policies — 60. Agents were paid a large commission the first year after a policy was purchased and then a smaller commission for nine more years. And that next year, Hal had 260 clients and would generate 2,560 names!

Hal retired a wealthy man.

COUNTERINTUITIVELY, HOW TO SOLICIT UNSOLICITED REFERRALS

I believe in the 1% Solution®, which means that if you improve by just 1 per cent a day, in 70 days you're twice as good! (If you don't believe it, work it out on your calculator: $1 \times 01 \times 70 = 2$.)

These next few pages may well be the '1% Solution' for you.

'Soliciting unsolicited referrals' may sound like an oxymoron, but it is not. I send people to my solicitor, doctor, dentist, designer, lawn maintenance company, car dealer, insurance broker and estate agent all the time but they don't ask me to do it. They don't provide a 'finder's fee' or gift (though I often get a 'thank you' note, but not always, nor do I expect one). Similarly, I have people referred to me by those same professionals as well as my clients, colleagues and friends.

If you think about this phenomenon for a few seconds, you'll realize you've probably been on both side of the equation as well. Sometimes, you haven't even been asked! At dinner, a friend will mention that they're going to try skiing and you mention your favourite ski shop, or they're going on holiday and you provide your favourite resort. (And, of course, you and I have also warned people where not to go, with whom one should never do business and whom not to trust.)

MASTERFUL INSIGHTS

Unsolicited referrals are provided proactively and reactively in the honest belief that we want to share quality, good experiences and success. That is a genuine and important motivation to encourage.

Note that we don't (usually) engage in this for personal ego needs, more out of a sincere desire to help. Some of the finest books we've read, most enjoyable holiday destinations and most wonderful meals originated with recommendations from people we trust and who we know have the requisite experience. In fact, with some plans, we make sure to consult with certain of our favourite 'experts' who have 'been there and done that'.

When someone gives us consistently bad advice, we don't ask again. Consequently, we ourselves are careful to provide good advice and not just guesses.

These referrals to our services involve zero cost and no marketing efforts whatsoever, right? Well, not quite. So, here's your 1% Solution. Here's how to create unsolicited referrals for your business:

1 Don't just provide high-quality work (which is a no-brainer) but make sure your buyer knows about it. Debrief regularly and demonstrate that you've been integral to the progress and success. Your buyer is the one with the peer-level contacts you need.
2 Generate new intellectual property weekly. It doesn't have to be breakthrough thinking, just incrementally better. Put this into public access, both to clients and non-clients (e.g., blog, newsletters, articles, videos, podcasts and so forth).

3 Invite your clients to your 'marketing' events. In other words, make sure there is a healthy mix of clients and prospects in workshops, at speeches, in Zoom calls, on interactive social media. Enable evangelism to happen. We actually try for a 50:50 mix.

4 Counterintuitively, perhaps, focus on your 'second tier' clients. In other words, these are good clients, but not your best clients. Yet they're happy and already trust you. It's not a huge leap for them to hear from your best clients and decide to join those ranks themselves. An ideal way to boost this, by the way, is through case studies.

The longevity, growth and success of professional services firms is directly dependent on the ability to solicit 'unsolicited referrals'.

8

SUCCESS, FAILURE AND THE MEDIOCRE

THE ALCHEMY OF VALUE-BASED MARKETING

The alchemy around being a masterful marketer is really quite simple. It's the value-based content you create, the credibility someone appreciates on your website and their ability to engage, establish rapport and feel like they are part of your community. People want to feel as though you have helped them, they can trust you and that you care. They do not want to feel that they have been marketing targets. They want to feel that when they consume your marketing, it is valuable, useful and insightful. People are looking for leaders and yet few are really stepping into a leadership role as an aspect of their marketing.

In Figure 8.1 you can see that the first step in our 'alchemy' is awareness and understanding of what need you are providing assistance and resolution. This may be a long-term and 'evergreen' need (talent acquisition) or a need you create (enabling the customer to buy), or an anticipated need (customers designing their own clothes

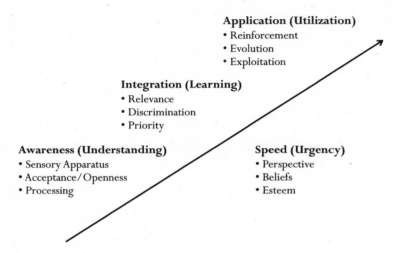

Application (Utilization)
- Reinforcement
- Evolution
- Exploitation

Integration (Learning)
- Relevance
- Discrimination
- Priority

Awareness (Understanding)
- Sensory Apparatus
- Acceptance/Openness
- Processing

Speed (Urgency)
- Perspective
- Beliefs
- Esteem

FIGURE 8.1 Strategic Marketing

as they now do with some vehicles). This is processed through sight and sound (the sensory apparatus) and sometimes through kinetics or even olfactory. (Certain smells remind us of pleasurable experiences, just as certain music does.)

This can create familiarization and openness, which leads to integration and learning. The need created must be relevant to the recipient (not merely pleasurable or rational), be distinctive and constitute a priority. Obviously, the search here is for visceral, emotional reactions which create an urgency to move forward. At that point, we can introduce application which encourages exploration and reinforcement. This is what happens with a house tour, or a test drive, or a 'no questions' return policy for shoes or clothing. It's what Apple did brilliantly by donating so many computers to schools beginning as early as the 1980s.*

Finally, note that all of this has an underpinning of speed. We want the customer's esteem to be high, perceptions to be positive and beliefs compatible with the product or service. Speed is as important as content in strategic marketing. People who delay decisions to engage in logical, rational analysis have a much lower rate of purchase than those who act on impulse or even those who feel that they have sufficient information even though they realize it isn't complete.

MASTERFUL INSIGHTS

Marketing takes people through a series of steps that, ideally, are symbiotic and encourage both acceptance and speed. Acceptance without speed is like dancing with no music.

You need to be nimble, energetic and innovative. Here's a good example ... For many years, American Express used the tagline, 'Don't leave home without it.' However, once the COVID-19 pandemic hit in 2020, no one was

---

*Calculate, if you can, how much internet sales would decline if you couldn't receive merchandise which was returnable for credit and/or refund. This is why there are so many disputes over services which can't be readily 'returned'.

leaving home! Amex changed the phrase in a great deal of its promotion to, 'Don't live life without it.' This accommodated the millions of card holders who were sitting in front of their computers ordering everything from bread and milk to furniture and entertainment online. All that took was a few words, reminiscent of the famous 'rinse and repeat' on shampoo labels, which immediately doubled the use of the product at zero additional cost to the manufacturer.

Amex is like supertanker ploughing through the waters, not a speedboat making turns on a dime. Yet it was able to significantly change its appeal by examining the conditions and its message and positioning.

In all probability, you are closer to a speedboat than a supertanker. Your marketing should never be a sacred totem or writ that is never disturbed but rather an organic pursuit that can change readily as conditions merit.

Here are some factors to be sensitive to which could impact your marketing:

- Technology: What changes have occurred, are occurring or will occur that can improve your marketing, change the way to reach your ideal buyers and improve responsiveness? No one anticipated the internet, but worse, many people failed to take advantage of it until they were far behind.

- Social mores: How have society's beliefs and values shifted or are likely to shift? You need to continually consider who your ideal buyers really are and what appeals to them. Organizations using 'sweat shop' labour in other countries have felt the justifiable backlash, as have those found creating hostile workplaces for women and minorities.

- Demographics: Your ideal buyers can shift and may surprise you. It's estimated that there were about 90,000 centenarians in 1995, there are about 450,000 today and there will be 3.7 million by 2050.

- Financial: As we write this, the largest transfer of wealth in history is taking place in the US as the 'Baby Boomers' of President Ronald Reagan's IRA legislation will be passing trillions of dollars on to the next generation, to charities and to other causes. We've seen both a Great Recession and a huge market boom within the past 12 years.

- Lifestyle: People are no longer compared to each other, but to the best and the beautiful, the wealthy and the physically fit, thanks to mass media and normative pressures. What is the role of your products and services in this fickle consumer economy? A treadmill doesn't really compare to a virtual trainer urging you on in the mirror.

SEVEN REASONS YOU'RE NOT GETTING ALL THE LEADS

There's a number of reasons why you may not be getting leads. The ones identified here are the most common:

1 You're a best-kept secret.
2 Your buyers are staying dark.
3 You're not making enough noise.
4 You're way too humble.
5 Your website is scaring people away.
6 You're not clear on who your buyer is.
7 You're not asking for them.

You're a best-kept secret

When they say you're a 'best-kept secret', what that really means is you're not being of service to as many people as you could be because your potential buyers don't know you exist. There is no value in being a best-kept secret unless you're guarding Air Force Hangar 52 in the Nevada Desert.

If you own a business, you're in the business of marketing and the effectiveness of your business's growth and longevity are directly tied to your ability to successfully market and establish both visibility and credibility. The best way to stop being a best-kept secret is to become more prolific and to increase the volume on your marketing dramatically.

MASTERFUL INSIGHTS

If you don't blow your own trumpet, there is no music.

Your buyers are staying dark

If your buyers aren't talking about you, one of two things is happening. Either you're not delighting them with the product or service you offer, or they mistakenly think you don't need more business. (Of course, the more paranoid might not want to share you and lose your attention.)

If your buyers are transient, meaning you are unable to retain them long term, you likely have a service delivery issue that needs to be rectified. If you're not regularly getting your buyers great results and hearing how pleased they are with your work, there is likely an opportunity for you to grow and improve OR they're not 'in the loop' and learning of your contributions.

Being busy is both a blessing and a curse and if you're always talking about how busy you are, you could be inadvertently telling your buyers that you are too busy for referrals. It's a good idea to regularly let your buyers know you're always happy to help their friends, family members, suppliers, customers and colleagues if they think your product or service can be of value.

You're not making enough noise

Thought leaders think 'out loud' and they verbalize their opinions on topics related to their industry. They speak, record videos, publish books, articles and blogs, make predictions and are regularly visible to others. They're not sitting quietly waiting for browsers to find them, they are making noise, in masterful and valuable ways, so their buyers discover them.

If you're not producing some form of content at least once a week, and if you're not distributing your content through some type of marketing channel daily, you're not making enough noise to attract attention.

CASE STUDY

A very provocative and controversial friend of mine, Randy Gage, was chatting with me about the critique we both get whenever we rock the boat. We agreed that *any* feedback is a sign of being heard and that apathy is the real enemy.

We compared and contrasted some of the unusual and creative 'attacks' that our speaking and writing drew and how it was so rewarding to roil the waters.

'Let's face it,' Randy observed, 'if we're not pissing off someone, somewhere, every day, we're just not doing our jobs!'

You're way too humble

It isn't bragging if it's true. Browsers and buyers have one big thing in common: they are looking for results. If you're not regularly talking about accomplishments you've had and those your buyers have had, you're missing an opportunity to demonstrate social proof. These are often the 'war stories' we discussed earlier (*see also* pp. 104–5).

This isn't about being 'Pinterest Perfect' and trying to construct an impression that isn't true. We're not talking about filters and reviews; what we mean here is that you should be more than a wee bit shameless about your success.

When you talk about your success, you allow others to see what is possible for them and you give them the courage to do the same. So stop hiding the great work you do and hoping someone will share it for you – they won't (or they just might take credit for it themselves).

Your website is scaring people away

Your website is a primary credibility source and it is also the 'stranger zone' where you must make a stellar first impression for those people who don't know, like and trust you yet. If you have website shame, if you cringe when you think about what a buyer or recommender might be thinking when they click on your homepage after having learned of you, it's time to stop having something that could belong in the Museum of Natural History.

You only get one chance to make a great first impression and in a digital world, your website is often where that happens. Ensure your website is modern, easy to read, has clear calls to action and that the message lets your buyers know immediately what you do and how you can help them. No one wants to guess, it's your job to remove the guesswork from your copywriting. Clever doesn't convert browsers into buyers, clear does.

You're not clear on who your buyer is
There are two ways you can ask for leads: one is relatively easy, the other requires a bit more courage. The easy way to ask for leads is to build in deliberate and clear calls to action on every page of your website. You need to know, with 100 per cent certainty, what action you want a browser to take and then you must do everything in your power not to confuse them. This confusion occurs when you offer too many calls to action and leave your browsers wondering what their first step should be.

If you want them to call you, say so. If you want them to email you, say so. And if you want them to fill out a form, make it perfectly clear that's what they should do. Your call to action is not a dinner menu. Don't give people too many choices, give them one. And when they do reach out, be responsive.*

Some people set up so much automation and so many different paths to generate leads and then they forget to pay attention to the inbound requests and respond regularly. If you tell people on social media to send you a private message, for example, you should check your messages and respond to them daily. The same goes for voicemail and email — and email includes your spam folder! Not checking your spam folder on a daily basis is a rookie mistake. And if you're feeling brave, get into the habit of asking your buyers for referrals.

DECONSTRUCTING THE EXPERTS AND REINVENTING THEIR WHEEL

Success leaves clues. If you want to be successful in your marketing, it's a good idea to deconstruct what other successful people have done. Top brands like Mercedes often 'deconstruct' or 'reverse engineer' their competitors' products in order to gain insights into their own success.

Most masterful marketers are early adopters when it comes to content creation, but they don't chase shiny objects. They also recognize that one format, or one way

---

*When you do decide to give options, give three, which provides choice but not confusion. More than three will cause paralysis in decision making, which is why when people are given a multitude of investment options they tend to just leave their money in low-interest bank accounts.

of producing content, greatly minimizes their ability to be found, and they have the courage and confidence to try new things without worrying about perfection.

Masterful marketers create content regularly. You can depend on them to write books, blog, record videos and podcasts, and adopt new technologies like Zoom, online forums and membership sites for programs they create for their communities. If you are fearful of technology and the advances it provides for your marketing, you will lag behind and you run the risk of having browsers think you're not current or relevant in how you show up.

While you might think the social audio app Clubhouse is a waste of time, you'd be wrong to dismiss the value of podcasting, something Alan has done for years now.[*] (And Alan does think Clubhouse is a waste of time, like a bad bar with lousy food, cheap liquor and a rowdy crowd. Depending on when you're reading these words, it may not even exist now.)

Experts evaluate the medium and ask themselves if this is a place where their buyers might hang out. You'll notice that while Alan has a podcast, he is not on the instant messaging app Snapchat, which makes perfect sense because that's not where his buyers are.

---

[*]The Uncomfortable Truth®, found at alanweiss.com

QUICK TUTORIAL:

What do your buyers read? Publish there.
What do your buyers attend? Speak there.
Where do your buyers hang out? Network there.
To whom do your buyers listen? Get on those radar
screens.

While it is relatively simple to model what successful
marketers do, actually having the self-discipline to do
so is another thing. When you're staring at a camera,
or a blank page, it can feel difficult to start but if you
get in the habit of constantly listening and looking for
ways to add value and keep asking yourself 'How can I
use this?', you'll find ideas for content creation are all
around. The idea is to create a body of work that reaches
far and wide, but you cannot do that if you only create
when you 'feel' like it and if the volume of work you do
create is sparse.

The Wheel
It helps if you think of your marketing as a wheel and that
wheel has several spokes. Each of the spokes represents an
area of marketing that is important for your marketing to
move you forward towards the attainment of the results
you wish to achieve. There are five spokes you want to

consider as part of the wheel that influences your marketing. Those spokes are:

- Your brand;
- Your content;
- Calls to action;
- Your social reach;
- Your attraction factor.

Your Brand

Your brand creates that first impression people have of you and while you may not look to your personal brand the same way as, say, Armani, there are many things that you can do to make your brand stronger. While these small details may not seem like a big deal to you, they go a long way towards helping you build trust and to develop a recognizable look and feel associated with you.

1 Use *current* photos of you, photos that really look like you when someone meets you in person.
2 Use the same fonts and colour schemes throughout your website.
3 Master your voice, or the *Martial Arts of Language*,[*] and keep your materials clean and easy for the user to read.

---

[*]Alan's ebook, available on his site: https://alanweiss.com/shop/books/the-martial-arts-of -language/

4 Make your website navigation intuitive for others and your content well organized and easy to find.

5 Apply the same look, feel and voice to everything you do, on your website, on social media channels and in any offline marketing elements such as slide presentations.

Your Content

Your content needs to provide your browsers and buyers with value. And you should showcase your personality and expertise in a variety of formats. Not only should your content be strong but it should also be optimized so that when people are searching for it, they can actually find it!

1 Don't just write, write so well people will want to read what you've written.

2 Use visuals, headings and sub-headings to make it easy for people to scan and read your content.

3 Remember the user experience in all you do and adapt your content to make it user-friendly. For example, don't have paragraphs that have 20 lines of text, or website font that is 8.0.

4 Use multiple formats, start adding video and audio content to the mix.

5 Use great imagery that is aligned with your brand.

QUICK TUTORIAL

'Writer's block' is a myth no less so than the Loch Ness Monster. It's simply an excuse for procrastination. Type a letter on your keyboard, then a few more to form a word. Now type more words to form a sentence. Now add more sentences to form a paragraph. Hit 'return' for a new paragraph and repeat. Voilà, you're writing!

Calls to Action

What do you most want browsers to do when they visit your website? Whatever you want them to do is what your call to action should be. You may have multiple types of calls to action on your website but you shouldn't have multiple calls to action on each page, otherwise you'll confuse people and they won't take any action at all.

Here are some calls to action you may want to consider:

1 Call or schedule a call. This can be done by providing a phone number, a fillable form or by providing a contact email address.
2 Download this. This is usually a free download where you are asking your visitor to provide an email address to receive a highly valued piece of content from you.

3 Register now. This could be a call to action to register for a free or paid webinar or online event.

4 Buy now. This is a very direct call to action that lets your audience know they can buy something from you. Usually associated with items in your shopping cart.

5 Subscribe. This is usually used when you want someone to subscribe to your mailing list or your podcast.

CASE STUDY

Alan always hated 'pop-up' menus, but Lisa convinced him to try them out so he created 11 points for success that is offered after someone is on his site for about 10 seconds. The response has been enormous, to the point where people write to thank him for the tremendous, free value.

These people keep coming back and buying.

Your Social Reach

Your social reach is dependent on the channels you choose to distribute your content. There are new social media channels popping up daily, which means you have to decide which ones are the most important for you to be found on.

Not only should you be found on these channels, but you should publish on them daily. The most popular channels at the time of writing this book are Facebook, LinkedIn, Instagram, YouTube for hosting video and Clubhouse for live audio.

The most popular types of content for sharing right now include:

- Long-form written posts;
- Video content;
- Audiograms;
- Branded documents;
- Swipe-able content mostly used on Instagram and LinkedIn.

Note that we would expect these to change frequently, so don't be confined to this list.

MASTERFUL INSIGHTS

When you invite a guest on your podcast, don't 'interview' the guest, nor promote the episode as an interview. The interviewer is usually 'subordinate' to the interviewee. Instead, position it as 'a conversation with …' so that you're co-equal and are peers. This builds your brand instantly.

Your Attraction Factor

Your attraction factor is important. People do business with people they know, like and trust. They have to like you if you want them to pay attention to you, otherwise they are going to hide your content or remove your connection to their feed.

Being likable doesn't mean you have to change who you are and worry about what other people think. It means you have to have people skills and know how to develop rapport with others.

You need excellent social skills when it comes to listening and responding to others. Learn how to acknowledge people and make them feel good in your presence. You also need to learn how to agree to disagree, which seems to be harder and harder to do online these days. A very sound option is not to respond at all to instigators and provocateurs.

9

HOW ISN'T THE ANSWER

START TODAY, CREATE VALUE-BASED CONTENT AND
DON'T OBSESS OVER TECHNOLOGY
How do you start without obsessing over technology?

Pick a format and go deep
As we've discussed, the three most common formats are
writing, recording audio or recording video. Pick which-
ever one of those formats is the easiest for you and get
started.

Sit down and brainstorm a list of questions that buyers
have asked you, and questions they should ask you, related
to your industry and make a list of topics you can create
content about.

Schedule time to do the work and stick with it
If it's writing, you may want to set aside 30–60 minutes
each day to write. Writing is a bit like a fly wheel – at first
it's hard to get the words flowing on the page but once you

get started, it gets easier to do. If you choose to write, do not self-edit as you go. This is the biggest single obstacle to progress in writing. Writing should be step one, editing to improve your written work should be step two and, preferably, done by someone else. Remember, this is all about success, not perfection.

If it's recording audio, you will still need to write some key points to guide you. Think about this in the same way as you would when you speak at an event — you typically prepare some notes or slides in advance that you can speak from. Do the same here and avoid reading what you are saying; just have a conversation with the listener. Your personality is also part of what is attractive to buyers so give yourself permission to reveal it. It's difficult to show your true personality if you're focused on reading the details written in a sentence.

If you're recording video, unless you've got the right equipment to do this well and you are extremely self-motivated to record, the best way to start is to hire a local videographer and record a few sessions at one time. If you prepare a list of topics and talking points, a videographer should be able to spend a day with you and record up to ten short videos that you can use weekly for the next ten weeks. When you do this, the videographer can also make any necessary edits to the videos for you.

Find someone to do the tech work for you if this isn't your strength
For blog writing, you want someone who can set up a blog in WordPress, optimize your writing for SEO, add images and proofread for you. Typically, when you hire someone to help you with blog set-up, they are also able to help you create a newsletter where you can also send what you have created to your mailing list with ease.

MASTERFUL INSIGHTS

Invest in technical help where you need it, this isn't the place to economize. Lights, sound, editing are all important because amateurism here will under-mine your message. If you don't believe that, watch the videos on LinkedIn, where people have their hair in their eyes, informal attire and a background that makes it seem as if a plant is growing out of their heads.

For audio, you can record with Zoom, or GarageBand, or use a recording program designed for podcasting. Then you will use a podcast hosting platform like Libsyn to host your recording and broadcast to podcast channels like Apple Podcast, Google Podcast, Stitcher and so forth. Once you do this, you will need someone to embed an audio player onto your website so visitors can listen there, too. Typically, people will use a blog roll install for the podcast and add the audio player, show notes and in some cases, resources and/or a transcript.

For video, you'll need someone to load your final videos to your YouTube channel, add descriptions, keywords and thumbnails, and then have them embed the video onto your website using the embed code generated by YouTube, usually on your blog with some copy to go along with the video. While this sounds difficult to do, it is not. If you can copy and paste, you can embed code and add a video to your website or to a blog post if you decide you want to do this yourself.

Create a schedule around creation and distribution

Once you choose the format you want to use, you should stick with it for at least 90 days and give yourself time to improve, be consistent and develop a process that works well for you. If it's working well, you typically have content that has been created in advance and it's getting easier (and much faster) for you to create.

Create a schedule around ongoing creation and the same for distribution. For example, if you want to publish a blog every Thursday, you should have it written and ready to be set up at least a week in advance (and, preferably, have a few 'in the bank'). Then if you publish on Thursday, you could email your mailing list with the blog on Friday and start sharing the information on social media. The key here is to be consistent. Alan's Monday Morning Memo comes out on Monday, not Tuesday. Pick a publishing date and stick to it as though the life of your business depends on it.

When it comes to distributing your content on social media, you'll want to 'mine' your content for powerful messages that you can use as hooks to interest browsers and buyers in reading, listening or watching more. This means you can't only share the information once; you need to have a schedule you follow that ensures you have something of value to share every single day, at least once.

Once you have this working well for one format, it's time to consider what else you can do and/or how you can build on what you've already created.

Add a new format and repeat process
Adding a new format can be content that is completely different from your first format, or it might be a repurposed version of the first format. Videos can have the audio ripped to become a podcast, while audio can be transcribed to become a blog post. You can also take the points from a blog, record a video on the same topic and then use the audio for a podcast.

When you add a new format, keep in mind that the goal is to provide value to the people who follow your work. Think about different ways to say the same thing on the topic you've focused on before. For example, you could write a blog on seven strategies for agile consulting and then use each of those seven strategies as a single tip on a video; you could record a podcast and only discuss five of the strategies or add three more and make it ten.

Think about your content's format like an ingredient in a recipe. Eating chicken on its own is boring, but when you take chicken and make different things with it, it's suddenly not so dull. You can make chicken salad, chicken fajitas or butter chicken, but it's still chicken. It's the way you prepare it that changes the experience for the person eating the chicken and the same principle is true for repurposing your content.

DISCRETIONARY TIME IS THE TRUE DEFINITION OF WEALTH

Don't fall into the trap of trying to do it all yourself. It is important that you recognize the value of your time and what tasks and activities can only be done by you and hire other people to help you with the rest. The biggest barrier to growth in your business can occur when you spend too much time doing things better done by other people.

You also can't create wealth or discretionary time if you're spending all your waking hours in the weeds, trying to figure out how to use technology unrelated to your line of work. If the air-conditioning unit needs to be fixed in your home, you hire a professional — you don't take time away from revenue generating activities in your business to learn how to fix air-conditioning units. The same is true for the technology side of marketing. Learn to discern what you must do and what someone else can do for you.

People actually think they're better off using software to file their taxes or an online service to apply for trademarks. This is insanity. Wouldn't you tell a client who says, 'We can set our own strategy,' that they need a professional — like you — and can't trust something that special and critical to a management team whose expertise is really in widget production?

CASE STUDY

I was hired by Mercedes-Benz North America to help them raise their service standards, since they were receiving far too many complaints about local dealerships. My first visit was to meet the vice president for North American Operations — my buyer reported to him.

He immediately began by telling me what he wanted me to do, where, in what manner and in what time frame. It was Teutonic discipline on steroids. I politely (I thought) stopped him.

'Excuse me, but I'm tripping over auto experts as I walked down the hall to your office, but no service experts and customer service experts. That's why you need me. So here's our deal: I won't tell you how to make brake pads, but you don't tell me how to consult.'

He stared at me for a good 20 seconds, gruffly said, 'Okay,' and off I went. And, yes, I solved the problem in a tenth of the time it would have taken them because the answer was in plain sight. They had superb dealership service in some locations, so I focused on them, created 'internal best practices' and we spread those to everyone else in the operation.

The Vice President became a source of glowing referrals.

One of the primary reasons we try to do too much ourselves and sacrifice precious discretionary time is that we have a *poverty mentality.*

In Figure 9.1 you'll see that we tend to move from our business inception to a position of abundance, from left to right. We need to slam and secure the 'watertight doors' on our personal and business success so that we don't slide back. (Once you're making a healthy profit, don't continue to resist investing in your people, for example.) Do you know people who, although very successful and happy to tell you about it, don't pick up the bill, don't volunteer,

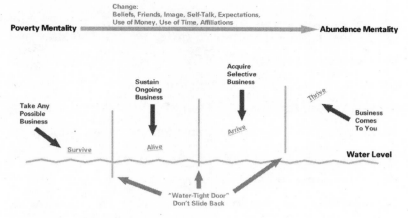

FIGURE 9.1 The Watertight Doors

don't share, don't mentor, don't ever put themselves out? They're still operating on the left, in a 'survival' mode, even though their business is well beyond it.

I've had people tell me in two consecutive sentences that they're having a record year but can't afford to invest in themselves or their development. This is why people continue to do things they should be outsourcing – to save a few bucks. But they're spending their discretionary time to do it. Thus, a great many people chase money so vehemently that they actually erode their real wealth.

MASTERFUL INSIGHTS

I can always make another dollar, but I can't make another minute.

Your marketing has to be savvy and you have to 'give to get' – that is, invest money in order to save you time and preserve your real wealth. Have you *ever* installed a carpet or painted a wall, or repaired your car as well as a professional in those fields could? Don't bother lying, the answer is 'no', just as no senior management team should be spending time devising a compensation system or choosing office furniture. They can *approve* the recommendations, but someone else should be making them and implementing them.

Masterful Marketing is about leveraging others' talents as appropriate.

NO ONE CAN REPLACE YOUR EXPERTISE, BUT A TEAM CAN ALWAYS HELP PROMOTE IT

Your expertise is uniquely yours. It is what differentiates you from anyone else who does what you do. (*See also* Figure 6.2, The Accelerant Curve. Your 'vault' contains that uniqueness.) The experiences and knowledge you have gained over this lifetime cannot be shared by someone who hasn't lived them. This is why you cannot abdicate responsibility for the creation of your thought leadership to someone else: it belongs to you and you alone. You can, however, hire a team to help you distribute your expertise through Masterful Marketing and help you to optimize your thought leadership in ways you may not have considered.

Anna Levesque, named one of the most inspirational paddlers around by *Canoe and Kayak* magazine, once wrote, 'Two young fish were swimming happily along in the ocean doing their thing. As they rounded the corner of a reef, an older and wiser fish swims by and cheerily asks them: "How's the water today?" One of the young fish looks puzzled, turns to her friend and asks: "What's water?"'

This is a great metaphor for how experts and thought leaders often behave when it comes to their work. They think everyone knows what they know, but in reality, they don't. And even if they know some of what you know, their capacity to explain it and contextualize it is very different from yours. The same is also true for a team that understands more about marketing than you do.

Typically, thought leaders go through three phases when it comes to marketing. First, they try to do everything themselves and that's when they get overwhelmed and realize that their time is better spent elsewhere. Second, they hire help, but usually their first hire is a junior person who requires a lot of support and direction, and while they may not be doing the marketing work themselves, they start to feel like they've hired an employee who needs to be managed and that's not always the best use of time, either. Third, they will look to hire a firm that has a team of marketing experts with a wide range of expertise, who can help with their brand, website, the publishing and distribution of content and more.

MASTERFUL INSIGHTS

'Doing it yourself' isn't always fastest, cheapest, more effective or most fulfilling. Other than that, it's great.

When you finally decide to hire a team to help you with your marketing, there are five things you should take into consideration:

Strategy

The strategy should support your business goals and objectives, long-term. Marketing takes time. When you hire a team to support you it is important that they understand the long-term goals for you and your business in order to effectively guide your marketing initiatives. This team should also have a clear understanding of who your buyer is, how you help them and be great at identifying new and innovative ways to get you in front of those people.

Outcomes and Objectives

All marketing should have a measurable return, but in order for you to have that, you need to know what the outcomes are that you're looking for. There are many parts to a marketing strategy and while your ultimate outcome may be sales, prior to acquiring a new piece of business you need to increase your visibility, increase traffic to your website and generate a lead. These are all interconnected and take time. Know what the ultimate outcome is for you and how you will measure that with a pre-defined objective and continue to guide your team to work towards that end result.

Marketing Tactics

Once the outcomes and objectives are clear, the team should be able to prioritize the best approach to Masterful Marketing for you. They should be able to recommend what marketing channels are most effective for you and what types of content format are best for your buyers and browsers. This team should also be on the cusp of what is working right now and guide you on best practices for your marketing. Depending on how aggressive your goals are will determine the volume and frequency of the marketing you need. The volume and frequency of marketing will impact the budget you will need for the team to do this work.

Return on Investment

Everyone wants an ROI from their marketing and yet it is often hard to quantify because there are so many variables where your marketing directly and indirectly affects a browser's decision to contact you. One of the things you can consider when looking at this ROI is the lifetime value of a new piece of business. If, for example, the lifetime value of a new piece of business is $100,000 and after 12–24 months you have gained several new buyers, then it stands to reason your investment (assuming it's less than the value of one new buyer) is a wise one.

Partnership

While it is tempting to hire a team and then ignore your marketing, that's not the most effective way to garner the results you want. A marketing team should work in partnership with you, the thought leader, and you should regularly inspect what you expect and provide the team with feedback and ask them what else you could be doing. The more you work in partnership (not micromanagement), the more effective their work will be.

View all this as leveraging your expertise and capitalizing on it, not replacing or outsourcing it! If we don't blow our own trumpet, there is no music. Think what happens when we have a very expert orchestra playing the music constantly and appealingly.

BE WILLING TO STRIKE OUT ENOUGH TO HIT A LOT OF BALLS OUT OF THE PARK

Remember the stack of paper example? Every piece of content, every piece of marketing is piling up over time and you stand tall as a thought leader on all of it. Some of the pieces in that pile are going to be duds. There will be pieces of content that no one commented on, ideas, programs and services that you tried to get off the ground that didn't work. But don't let that stop you. It's the accumulation of these things and the knowledge you gain from what works and doesn't work that will help you hit it out of the park eventually.

MASTERFUL INSIGHTS

Never give up. Alan's best-selling, 30-year — and now in its sixth edition — book, *Million Dollar Consulting*, was rejected 15 times before McGraw-Hill agreed to publish it. Now it's continually in the top ten consulting books on Amazon.

And just like the game of football or baseball, you should keep score and statistics so that you know what is and isn't working so you can adjust. Here's what you should measure and pay attention to: some of it is easy to track, but some you may need to track manually.

Social Reach

This is the number of people who are connected to you and your work. This includes those who are connected to your social media profiles and pages whether they are connections, friends, likes or followers. Be aware that the quality of social reach is dependent on how many ideal buyers and recommenders are included, not merely volume.

Engagement

This is the amount of engagement (likes, comments and shares) you receive on the marketing you distribute through social media. But it's very easy to hit a 'like' button or to 'react'. The key is whether those comments are generating enquiries into your business and offering.

Website Traffic

This is the amount of traffic that visits your website on a daily, monthly and yearly basis. The goal of marketing is to attract more traffic to your website to consume and read your body of work.

List Growth

This is the size of your mailing list growth. You should regularly be doing new things to attract people to your mailing list so you can communicate and share value with them regularly. You will find that the vast majority of leads join your mailing list before they reach out to you about doing business. Even a large list, if static and not growing (or 'churning', meaning new people are simply replacing departures) is less and less useful over time because it won't lead to as much business on your Accelerant Curve.

Leads

This is the number of people who reach out to you to enquire about doing business with you. When someone initiates contact with you, always ask them how they found out about you. This will help you to know what is effective in your marketing.

CASE STUDY

I was conducting an inexpensive workshop in Boston for people who might not be able to afford my usual offerings. (This is the left side of the Accelerant Curve and the session was priced at only $250.) I asked at the outset how each of the 200 people had heard of me. Exactly 190 had read a book I had written. The other ten had been referred to me by someone else who had read a book I had written.

You just have to ask. You don't need more elaborate or expensive investigation than asking people how they learned of you – people who are giving you money.

Don't fall for vanity metrics

While you should measure the effectiveness of your marketing, don't fall into the comparison trap or focus on vanity metrics that aren't relevant to you. If the average value of a new piece of business for you is $100,000, you don't need very many buyers to have a successful business. Also, you don't need 100,000 Instagram followers.

Vanity metrics are a tricky measurement of success – it's like measuring the popularity of a football or baseball player, ahead of their athletic performance. It can also mean that someone paid to gain all of those metrics when it comes to social media and what you're comparing to isn't really a true reflection of that person's influence or business success. Don't forget that people 'buy' names for their social media accounts, but more importantly, we know of no bank in the country that accepts 'likes' to pay the mortgage.

Recognize that success takes time and it won't be perfect all of that time. Babe Ruth's career spanned 22 seasons, 10 World Series, 714 home runs and 1,330 strikeouts. In 1923, he broke the record for the most home runs and the most strikeouts. He didn't let the number of times he struck out stand in the way of his success. In fact, you could make a case he wouldn't have had the success without the strikeouts, because he was swinging for the seats every at-bat. So, be like Babe Ruth: don't let the number of times you strike out stand in the way of becoming a world-class thought leader and masterful marketer.

Remember, 'How' isn't the answer, 'what' is the question.

What marketing avenues best suit your strengths?
What marketing avenues best reach your ideal buyers?
What are your buyers reading?
What are your buyers attending?
What are your buyers listening to?
What attracts your buyers to 'hang out'?

This isn't like the old Abbott and Costello routine, 'Who's on first?' It's about creating the value, not focusing on the technology (how), creating true wealth for yourself in discretionary time and not chasing money, and leveraging your marketing power with outside expertise where needed.

SURVIVAL OF THE EYEBALLS

IF PEOPLE DON'T SEE YOU, THEY WON'T KNOW, LIKE,
TRUST AND DO BUSINESS WITH YOU
You don't know who you don't know until you know who
they are, right?

If someone doesn't know you exist, you will never be
on their radar as an option so it's critical that masterful
marketers are always thinking about how they can be
seen by not only more people, but the right people (ideal
buyers). So how do you get seen (*and* heard)?

Here are six ways you can get more eyeballs on you and
your work:

Attend in-person events
There is no substitute for meeting and connecting with
people in person. There is something about the energy
and connection that take place in person that cannot be
replaced online. It can, however, be strengthened and trust
can be fast-tracked when you expand those connections to

include online and in-person interactions. There are three different types of event you can consider for meeting and connecting with people who are your ideal buyers.

The first is any event you host yourself. This can be a large or a small event where you invite a mixture of buyers and prospects to gather together. Such an event positions you as the host or leader and is a great way to establish credibility and provide value to your community.

The second is to speak at an industry event that your buyers attend. When you do this, you again position yourself as a leader and create an opportunity to meet people.

The third is to attend an event that would be valuable to your buyer. At this event, you can network and meet people, and you can even host your own micro-event within the event. A micro-event could be an intimate networking session you host in your suite, or a breakfast or dinner where you invite people to join you. Some hotels have an executive lounge and/or give you access to a private lounge where you can do this, too. It can be a great way to add value for others and build relationships away from the actual event.

Post content regularly

You've heard this before, but creating and sharing your content on a regular basis (at least weekly) and distributing it daily is an important way of getting eyeballs on your work. Posting and distributing content on your website and your own social media channels is one way and there are other ways to do this, too. For example, you can look for opportunities to guest-blog on someone else's website, write for an online magazine like *Thrive Global* or a blogging platform like Medium. Many print-based magazines also have an online presence where they publish content provided by guest experts. Some of these opportunities will be earned based on the body of work you've created and respect you've gained for your work, while others may be paid placements or advertorials.

MASTERFUL INSIGHTS

The Web has created a huge demand for spoken and written communications that isn't nearly being sated. Provide high-quality, unique content and you'll be in great demand.

Grow your network

Online technologies make it easier and faster than ever to grow your network and we're not talking about adding a bunch of 'friends or connections' that you don't know by simply clicking buttons on Facebook or LinkedIn. Your network is only valuable if people know who you are.

Here are some easy and effective ways for you to organically build a quality network that translates into real relationships and opportunities. While you can do this on any social network, LinkedIn is really the best platform to do this with if you want to keep track of effectiveness. LinkedIn allows you to see when people have got promoted or changed jobs and stay connected regardless of changes in email addresses.

Spend time connecting with the following people:

- Current and past clients;
- Any individual you've given a proposal to who didn't engage you;
- Current and former professional colleagues;
- People you meet at in-person events;
- People you buy from;
- Community leaders you'd like to know better;
- Friends you went to school with;
- Professional contacts (doctors, designers, accountants, attorneys, etc.).

As you build your network, look at who your connections are connected to. You will likely find people in their connection lists that you know personally as well. And while you may think that friends you went to school with decades ago aren't important, it's important to remember that people remember you based on the last impression they have of you.

If they thought you were great in high school, they likely still have that same memory of you. The point is your network and ability to expand your network should start with those you know and you should make it a point to continuously add people to your network with whom you still interact. However, it is better to have a smaller network of people who know, like and trust you than it is to have a larger network of people who have no idea who you are.

Comment on other people's content

If you want to meet new people, make it a habit to comment on other people's content at least one to three times each day. A large number of people share content publicly and by searching or following hashtags, you can participate in conversations and share your insights and opinions in places where people don't know you. By doing this, people start to notice you and if they see you regularly add value, they will reach out to you.

Commenting on other people's content to add value is a good idea. Don't comment to take away from what someone has shared, comment to contribute and add value. Remember, you want people to know, *like* and trust you, not know you and think you're a creep! (No one builds statues honouring critics or flocks to their doors with business.)

Pay attention to what your buyers post and follow relevant hashtags so you can find things to comment on and add value to.

Post videos, the best way

One of the best ways for people to get to know you and your work and resonate with you is through video. While most people don't love how they look on camera, it's not a good enough excuse not to shoot video if you want to be someone who is seen and seen as someone who adds value.

Video allows your personality to be appreciated. It allows you to provide value, demonstrate humility and provide humour. It's a great way for people to feel connected to you, even if they have never met you in person. If you're not producing video content on a regular basis, you're missing an opportunity to be seen.

Video is great and livestreaming is even better, because when you are livestreaming there is no editing or fixing what you say and how you show up. It's as close as you can get to speaking in front of a live audience at an event. Show up and do this regularly and over time, you will attract a loyal following of people eager to watch what you have to say.

Start a podcast

Audio is one of the fastest-growing communication channels online. The barrier to entry is low because people don't need to be concerned with lighting, editing, camera or background set up and/or how they look. (That's both a blessing and a curse. Audio can be way, way too informal. Just try Clubhouse.)

Podcasting has gained popularity and is also an excellent way to expand your network by hosting guest conversations with your ideal buyer. You can host your own solo shows for people to listen to and you can have conversations with a variety of different people to help expand your network.

You can record one podcast and distribute it to as many podcast platforms as you want instantaneously. Podcasts are consumed by many people on their mobile devices while they work, walk or commute to work, and most newer vehicles have podcast players built in for users to listen on the go.

If you're not comfortable on camera, podcasting allows you to read easily from a list of items you'd like to talk about and find your voice without the discomfort of being videotaped while you try to gather your thoughts.

In summary, you may not be comfortable in all media, but our advice is to start where you are most comfortable, create momentum and followers, and then move into less comfortable media. This is about success, not perfection. I leave most of my errors on the video, in the podcast, on the recording. Unless I've said something simply wrong, I don't mind correcting a word or laughing at my own bumbling. This makes us human. And it removes the stress of trying to show people you're perfect. This isn't about perfection but it is about excellence. I'd rather have excellent help that provides improvement rapidly than 'perfect' help, which is never quite ready to go on stage.

YOU DON'T NEED A HUGE AUDIENCE TO MAKE A HUGE IMPACT

You don't need 10,000 followers on Instagram and 100,000 on your mailing list to be successful (although, if they are all potential ideal buyers, it certainly doesn't hurt!). The people selling you on these beliefs are the people making money out of doing it – selling names or promoting techniques to acquire names.

Every business is different in terms of who the buyer is, the average lifetime value of a new piece of business and the cost of acquisition, which means that you should focus on what you need for your business and put blinders on for the rest. You *do* need an audience, that is true, but the size of that audience depends on unique variables related to your business. Don't let marketing generalizations distract you from what is most important.

Know what your lead source is, how long it takes someone to interact with you as a browser until becoming a buyer and what the long-term value of that buyer is. Know what your conversion rate is (how many conversations it takes to acquire one new buyer) and assess for yourself how many buyers (and therefore browsers) you really need to reach your goals.

A lead source may be someone who subscribes to your mailing list or is connected to you on LinkedIn. They may have heard a recording, watched a video, read an article or a book. They may consume your marketing materials for weeks or years before they make first contact. Once they make contact, it may require one or many conversations before it results in a sale.

Not all conversations will result in a sale, which is why understanding your conversion rate (per cent of browsers who become buyers) matters. It's also important to understand the lifetime value of each new buyer in order for you to really assess how big an audience you need. There's not a 'one size fits all solution' for every business.

FIGURE 10.1 From Lead to Lifetime Value

Audience and impact are not mutually exclusive. You can make a huge impact on the life of one person through generosity and being of service. You can also impact on a stranger's life who consumes your content and you might never know it happened. Knowing that you're making an impact is often the fuel that sustains creativity.

While we all know Alan is filled to the brim with confidence, not everyone is born that way. For those who are not, we encourage you to start an evidence folder. What is an evidence folder? It's a place where you store the positive messages, emails, cards and words of affirmation that show the impact you've made on the life of another person for those moments when doubt creeps in. (Actually, Alan has one – he calls it 'Rave Reviews' very theatrically.)

There will be days when you doubt your impact and question if what you're doing matters and is valuable to others. When you have an evidence folder, you can quickly remind yourself that you are making an impact and that impact is far more important than the size of your audience.

CASE STUDY

When George W. Merck founded the great American pharmaceutical company that still bears his name, he created an aphorism which was in the firm's value statements and beliefs ever after:

Do good and good will follow.

He believed that if you served customers and took care of employees well, profits would ensue. People didn't join Merck to make millions, as they might in a venture capital company. They joined because they believed in the mission: to bring the greatest in scientific research to the greatest areas of human health needs.

At one point, Merck developed a drug that turned out to be ineffective for the intent of the research. However, by accident, it turned out that it was a safe and efficacious cure for African River Blindness, the greatest cause of fatalities in Africa at the time.

Merck donated the drug to African governments and relief agencies and River Blindness was hugely reduced.* At the time of writing, Merck is #69 of the Fortune 500 and was once voted 'America's Most Admired Company' for five years in a row by CEOs in *Fortune* magazine's annual survey.

When our coaching clients are confused by client conditions, options and what to do next, we ask this simple question:

What's in the client's best interests?

---

*https://www.nytimes.com/1987/10/22/world/merck-offers-free-distribution-of-new-river-blindness-drug.html

That question is the express lane to the correct action. It's not about 'chasing money' or fame or being loved. It's about improving the client's condition. Our impact can be singular, one person at a time in coaching; or with groups, helping teams perform better; or organizationally in restructuring, strategy, talent management and so forth. Those are all choices we can make. However, there is no choice in terms of understanding our impact when it comes to the other person's well-being.

MASTERFUL INSIGHTS

Don't be fooled by numbers. Helping one person to help other people leverages what you do. That has huge impact. St Paul went from city to city preaching and telling others to spread the word. He was the world's first viral marketer.

You want the eyeballs on you not because you're a performing seal, but because you're providing unique value. Marketing is about the creation of need and as we've tried to explain to this point, most people know what they want but not what they need.

When we merely respond to people's 'wants' we are a commodity, usually competing on price for undifferentiated services. But when we create 'need' we are unique providers of improvement not perceived as available elsewhere.

BE WILLING TO DO WHAT MOST PEOPLE WON'T DO

A client of mine sent me an update on how the week had gone. She said that she had been focused on filling the pipeline because sales were slow. She had closed one new piece of business, a lead that came from LinkedIn after she had shared something of value the week prior. The irony was that she hadn't shared anything since.

Be consistent in your marketing and reflect on what is working and then do more of that! If you are inconsistent in your approach to building a business, your sales, revenue growth and impact will be inconsistent too.

This book came to fruition when Lisa emailed Alan on a Saturday afternoon and asked him if he'd consider writing a book with her. Alan, in typical Alan fashion, replied within the standard 90 minutes and said, 'Sure, send me the premise and chapter outline by Monday.'

Lisa spent the rest of the weekend doing the work so that Alan would take her seriously and has continued to do so up until the final chapter of this book you're reading right now. So be willing to ask for help and then be willing to accept help on your journey. Most people are afraid to ask for help and to take the action someone with more experience than they have suggests.

Look for experts, guides and trusted advisors on your journey and be willing to do what it takes — even when it feels uncomfortable, or not quite good enough yet. You learn by doing.

Invest in who you are becoming as an expert and thought leader. When you invest in your own growth and personal development, you can shortcut the time it takes to become the next 'version of yourself'. People often question the fee associated with investing in themselves, instead of looking at the value of that investment in terms of who they become and how that impacts not only their business but the experience their buyers enjoy with them.

There is no better return on investment than betting on yourself.

Completed imperfectly is better than perfectly never completed and the only way to improve is by doing. Don't hang onto your work, your dreams or ideas for too long or they will shrivel up. Those people who are willing to act fast, take risks and release ideas before they are perfect are the leaders and trailblazers making a difference in the world. Recognize that you can tweak and perfect as you go along, but don't wait: the time is now.

From our experience, we've estimated that about half of people who read a book or attend an event or watch a video or listen to a podcast are actually moved to action. You might blame a lack of impact from the source, of

FIGURE 10.2 Giant Ground Sloth

course (!), but that's not really the main reason. The main reason is sloth. Above is a representation of a giant ground sloth from the Pleistocene epoch. About four tons and 20 feet long, it remains one of the largest land mammals ever to have lived.

It was a huge creature, but very slow and vulnerable. And it has been extinct for millions of years!

Half of those people described above are slothful. They believe what they've learned, but they are in no hurry to implement it. It can wait. They have fires to fight and places to go.

Half of the remainder will make an attempt, but it won't be immediately successful, so they'll revert to old habits. It's too painful to depart the beaten track and they don't like the difficulty of implementing something new that doesn't provide instant gratification. The learning curve is flat.

The final half of this last group, however, about 12 per cent of the total, will make changes because they will invest the time and energy to implement. They are accustomed to accountability and discipline, might even join others in the attempt and are intent to gain the ROI on what they've spent on themselves. That's not a great percentage, but it does seem to us to be the sad truth. That's why it's important to help clients through the creating of initiatives and through the launch into routine, daily application of new approaches. They require the fresh air of our involvement to overcome the exhaust fumes from their own rituals.

When I ran the sprints in high school and lettered in track in my freshman year, the coach told me, 'Run *through* the tape. Picture the real finish line ten yards past the tape, otherwise you'll tend to ease off at the finish.' I learned to do that and beat some people faster than me by inches, because I was still running hard, leaning forward, and they were letting up, leaning backward.

Masterful Marketing means setting your sights past your goals, accepting success and not waiting for perfection, and being resilient to overcome inevitable setbacks and detours. Within these chapters we've tried to provide the ideas, skills, techniques and incentive to move forward and be successful. Yet, no one ever learned to ride a bike or ski by merely reading a book. You have to try it, often with a coach at your side, but always with a willingness to fail and learn with each setback. So we admonish you, in order not to be a giant sloth, not to become extinct:

- Choose three techniques from this book to implement which you think will most help your business and about which you're most passionate;
- Select one of those techniques and find an opportunity to apply it *now*;
- If it works, exploit it and begin using it constantly;
- If it doesn't work, examine what went wrong, learn from it and try it again;
- Once successful, move on to your next of the three;
- Rinse and repeat.

'Rinse and repeat' was one of the cleverest marketing techniques in history, doubling shampoo sales without a single investment. People don't need to shampoo twice, no one's hair is that dirty, but if an expert is suggesting it, why take a chance?

We're talking about something far more substantive here — value to your clients — but you're nonetheless the expert suggesting the value so shout it out!

And that should at least double your sales.

MASTERFUL INSIGHTS

To score, you have to get on base, which means you need a bat in your hand, standing at the plate. You might strike out, but you'll get more chances. If you're not in the game, or not even in the ballpark, you'll never score a run. In our profession, that means you'll never help anyone. That's not a legacy. So, hit the ball and run the bases. Get in the game!

ABOUT THE AUTHORS

Alan Weiss is one of those rare people who can say he is a consultant, speaker and author *and mean it*. His consulting firm, Summit Consulting Group, Inc., has attracted clients such as Merck, Hewlett Packard, GE, Mercedes-Benz, State Street Corporation, Times Mirror Group, the Federal Reserve, The New York Times Corporation, Toyota and over 500 other leading organizations. He has served on the boards of directors of the Trinity Repertory Company, a Tony-Award-winning New England regional theatre, Festival Ballet, chaired the Newport International Film Festival and been president of the board of directors of Festival Ballet Providence.

His speaking typically includes 20 keynotes a year at major conferences and he has been a visiting faculty member at Case Western Reserve University, Boston College, Tufts, St John's, the University of Illinois, the Institute of Management Studies and the University of Georgia Graduate School of Business. He has held an appointment as adjunct professor in the Graduate School of Business at the University of Rhode Island, where he taught courses on advanced management and consulting skills to MBA and PhD candidates. He once held the record for selling out the highest-priced workshop (on entrepreneurialism) in the then 21-year history of New York City's Learning Annex. His PhD is in psychology. He has served on the Board of Governors of Harvard University's Center for Mental Health and the Media.

Alan is also an inductee into the Professional Speaking Hall of Fame® and the concurrent recipient of the National Speakers Association Council of Peers Award of Excellence, representing the top 1 per cent of professional speakers in the world. He is a Fellow of the Institute of Management Consultants, one of only two people in history holding both those designations.

His prolific publishing includes over 500 articles and 60 books, including his bestseller, *Million Dollar Consulting* (McGraw-Hill), now in its 30th year and sixth edition. In 2021, he published *Legacy: Life is not about a search for meaning but the creation of meaning* (Routledge). His books have been on the curricula at Villanova, Temple University and the Wharton School of Business, and have been translated into 15 languages.

His career has taken him to 60 countries and 49 states (he is afraid to go to North Dakota). In an editorial devoted to his work *Success Magazine* cited him 'a worldwide expert in executive education'. The *New York Post* called him 'one of the most highly regarded independent consultants in America'. He is the winner of the prestigious Axiem Award for Excellence in Audio Presentation.

He is the recipient of the Lifetime Achievement Award of the American Press Institute, the first-ever for a non-journalist and one of only seven awarded in the 65-year history of the association. He holds an annual Thought Leadership Conference, which draws world-famous experts as speakers.

He has coached former candidates for Miss Rhode Island/Miss America in interviewing skills. He once appeared on the popular American TV game show *Jeopardy*, where he lost badly in the first round to a dancing waiter from Iowa.

Alan has been married to the lovely Maria for 52 years and they have two children and twin granddaughters. They live in East Greenwich, RI, with their dogs, Coco, a cavapoo, and Bentley, a white German Shepherd.

Lisa Larter is a business strategist, digital marketing expert, author and speaker. Her business, the Lisa Larter Group, helps clients to formulate marketing strategies that support their business goals and their objectives for increasing their visibility, leads and customer acquisition. Lisa provides consulting and advisory services as well as a full suite of implementation services that include social media and content management, book marketing campaigns and website design.

Lisa's background is in the wireless industry, where prior to starting her own business she helped one of Canada's largest telecommunication companies build-out their retail distribution channel, supporting a field team of over 1,000 people and 100 million in retail sales. She left that role in 2006 and opened her own retail 'bricks and mortar' business, which she sold in 2012.

She has successfully built two businesses with a turnover in excess of seven figures and has helped many of her clients reach the seven-figure mark, attract such clients and sell their own companies. A self-taught high school dropout, Lisa runs a business book club called Thought Readers, which was initiated to help others learn more so they can earn more.

Lisa recently launched her podcast, She Talks Business, where she shares the strategies that are necessary to start and scale your business beyond seven figures ... and keep it there.

INDEX

Note: page numbers in **bold** refer to diagrams.